The OLD MAGIC of Christmas

MARLENE RAEDISCH

About the Author

Linda Raedisch is an eclectic writer with an art background and an interest in the practical aspects of prehistory, history, and religion. Her first book is *Night of the Witches: Folklore, Traditions & Recipes for Celebrating Walpurgis Night*, and she is a frequent contributor to Llewellyn's annuals. She lives in northern New Jersey with her daughter, Mika; their gray cat; and a growing collection of brooms.

The OLD MAGIC of Christmas

Yuletide Traditions for the Darkest Days of the Year

LINDA RAEDISCH

Llewellyn Publications
Woodbury, Minnesota

FIRST EDITION
Sixteenth Printing, 2023

Book design by Donna Burch
Cover: iStockphoto.com/7855186/Vetta Collection/Stanislav Pobytov
Cover design by Ellen Lawson
Editing by Brett Fechheimer
Interior illustrations © Chris Down
Interior sleigh: Art Explosion

Library of Congress Cataloging-in-Publication Data

Raedisch, Linda, 1968–
The old magic of Christmas : yuletide traditions for the darkest days of the year / Linda Raedisch.—First Edition.
pages cm.
Includes bibliographical references and index.
ISBN: 978-0-7387-3334-0
1. Christmas–Folklore. [1. Christmas.] I. Title..

GT4985.R24 2013
394.2663—dc23

Llewellyn Publications
A Division of Llewellyn Worldwide Ltd.
2143 Wooddale Drive
Woodbury, MN 55125-2989
www.llewellyn.com

Printed in the United States of America

Other Books by This Author

Night of the Witches: Folklore, Traditions & Recipes for Celebrating Walpurgis Night

Acknowledgments

Special thanks go to Vivette Pilloton for the use of her library and for general moral support; Chris Gordon of Icepedition Tours for the use of his Icelandic collection; Chanda Yonzon for tea and childcare; Priya and Nilesh Shrestha for dinners and Czech support; Jaclyn Pien for coffee and crafting input; and especially to my mother, Marion Raedisch, for help in the kitchen and at the translating table, and for all those hours spent with the *Lutzelfrau*. Happy Christmas to all!

Contents

Listen! We are beginning our story!
When we arrive at the end of it we shall,
it is to be hoped, know more than we do now.

~HANS CHRISTIAN ANDERSEN, "THE SNOW QUEEN"[1]

1. All direct quotes from "The Snow Queen" are from my own crumbling, tartan-bound copy of *Tales from Hans Andersen* published by Thomas Y. Crowell & Co. in 1897. I suspect it of being an overly flowery, Victorian translation, but it is the one to which I am sentimentally attached.

Introduction

Christmas, at its heart, is a hazy thing. This book explores the finer points of how it came to be that way, without, it is to be hoped, actually dispelling any of that seductively glittering haze. If you are open to the experience of a deeper and, yes, darker season, if you're not afraid to open the door to the odd ghost or wizened witch, if you would welcome a shiver that has nothing to do with the coming of winter, then you've come to the right place. While this is not a children's book, it was written by a lover of fairy tales, and you will find scattered references to Hans Christian Andersen, C. S. Lewis, J. R. R. Tolkien, and a few others you might not immediately associate with Christmas. Meandering throughout are references to my favorite children's story of all, "The Snow Queen," in which the courageous young Gerda makes her way, sometimes barefoot, from an attic apartment in Denmark to a witch's garden, a robbers' camp, and on through Lapland to the "snow-saloon" at the heart of the Snow Queen's stronghold to effect the spiritual rescue of her playmate, Kay. "The

Snow Queen" is not, strictly speaking, a Christmas story, but the lands through which Gerda passes are in many cases the same lands through which the ancient Yuletide goddess has also passed with her retinue of fairies, ghosts, and goblins.

You don't have to be Christian to fall in love with the Christmas season. We've all seen those stickers urging us to "Keep the Christ in Christmas." I choose to interpret these in the most positive of lights, as a call to Christians to use the season as a means of more deeply exploring their faith. Pagans can do the same. Despite what you may have heard, the old gods and goddesses are not so easy to pick out in our modern festivities, but what a joy it is when you do spy one of them hanging around the punch bowl or riding in with the mistletoe. Such a lengthy season demands a cast of thousands, and witches, trolls, and household sprites all have their parts to play.

In these pages you will find elves aplenty, both light elves such as might be expected to have taken up employment as toymakers under the swaying curtain of the northern lights, and dark elves who lurk in the forest, hiding their faces from the sun. I propose that Yule, and the days leading up to it, is the best time to contrast our more recent conception of these earthbound spirits with the more interactive relationship our ancestors had with them in the past.

There is a popular belief among both Pagans and non-Pagans that Christmas as we know it is essentially a Pagan celebration, its rituals the richly dressed attempts of primal people to rekindle the dying embers of the sun. Though this is a fine mythology in itself, it's really only half the story. Some of the creatures you're about to meet are unabashedly heathen, while others are the products of highly Christianized imaginations. The vast majority are some combination of the two.

As you turn the pages of this book, I would like you to feel as if you are forcing open an ancient church door, to find not dusty pews but an old-growth forest, moonlight glancing off the holly leaves as gauzy spirits dart among the boughs. I hope you, the reader, will be as surprised as I was at some of the discoveries I have made in the course of my own journey through this forest. At first glance, the Swedish Lucia, with her crown of lights and blood-red sash, is a shoe-in for an ancient personification of—or sacrifice to—the sun, but this turns out not to be the case. (On St. Lucy's Day, you may also be surprised by what you find under the Bohemian Lucy's skirts!) Conversely, the Italian witch Befana, whose name means "Epiphany" and whose story is inextricably bound up with that of the Three Kings who brought gold, frankincense, and myrrh to the Baby Jesus, owes her existence as much to a Germanic goddess as to the Book of Matthew.

There is no denying that Christmas is and always has been largely about the choosing, buying, wrapping, and presentation of gifts. The Roman Saturnalia, an early precursor of our own holiday, was marked by the exchange of candles, little clay dolls, and other trinkets. Gift-giving is, after all, an expression of goodwill, especially when you are handing a little of your hard-earned cash back down the socio-economic ladder. No, you don't have to make merry, but you ought to take the time to remember that we are all, as Scrooge's nephew attempted to explain to his uncle, "fellow-passengers to the grave, and not another race of creatures bound on other journeys."

Which brings us, naturally, to the three Christmas ghosts familiar to the whole world: those of Past, Present, and Yet to Come. *A Christmas Carol* was neither the first nor the last Christmas ghost story Charles Dickens wrote. Nor did he invent the genre; he brought an already established storytelling tradition to new heights. Christmas and the spirit world were so closely linked in Dickens's imagination that he saved up his spookiest ideas for publication in December.

In the forging of our own bright, shiny American Christmas, certain attitudes, beliefs, and practices have been clipped away, for that is the nature of tradition. Some customs might survive for centuries while others bite the dust under the Christmas tree skirt almost as soon as they are born. Rather than let those old clippings lie in a heap on Santa's workshop floor, I have gathered a handful of them up and held their rough edges to the light. Take a look. While I cannot with any confidence promise you a merry Christmas, I can offer you the prospect of a very interesting one. Many of you may be of the opinion that Christmas is all about the kids. I disagree; Christmas is all about safely *scaring* the kids and sometimes ourselves in the process.

The Christmas season used to stretch all the way from late October to February 2. It should be noted that while the broom-toting Barborky appear predictably on St. Barbara's Eve (December 3) and La Befana can be counted on to sweep through the sky with her sack of toys on Epiphany Eve (January 5), there are few hard and fast rules when it comes to the order of this otherworldly procession. If I have placed a certain occurrence in a certain province on Christmas Eve, it does not mean that a similar ritual might not take place on New Year's Eve or Twelfth Night somewhere else. In the early Middle Ages, the Christmas season was reckoned to begin on November 1, but keep in mind that the medievals' November 1 was not our November 1.[2] What we now call Halloween was, for the ancient Celts, the night preceding the start of the winter half of the year and therefore a sort of New Year's Eve. And for the Anglo-Saxons, what we call the beginning of winter was "midwinter."

As in my first book, *Night of the Witches: Folklore, Traditions & Recipes for Celebrating Walpurgis Night*, many of the uncanny creatures you'll meet are Germanic in origin. But folk beliefs and traditions, like the people who create them, often flow smoothly one into another instead of falling into neat scholarly categories. Our journey into Christmas will

2. The 365-day year with which we are all familiar was invented by Julius Caesar, or someone working for him, in 46 BCE. This is the "Julian" or "Old Style" calendar. Because it does not take the earth *exactly* 365 days to complete its revolution around the sun, over the centuries a sort of seasonal drift occurred that not even the Julian leap year could correct. Finally, in 1582, Pope Gregory XIII, or someone working for him, removed ten days from the fall of that year and tinkered with the leap-year system to create the "Gregorian" or "New Style" calendar. The Gregorian calendar, which promises many of us a white Christmas each year, was accepted higgledy-piggledy throughout the Western world over a period lasting from 1582 to 1923. This should help explain why December 13, 21, and 25 have all been hailed at one time as the date of the winter solstice. When you also take into account the ecclesiastical calendar, the landlords' calendar, the Old Icelandic calendar, and the lunar calendar to which Easter obstinately clings, it's a wonder that there is any consensus at all when it comes to our modern holidays.

also take us deep into Celtic, Italic, Baltic, and Slavic lands. With such a wealth of characters on hand, one has to draw the line somewhere, and I have chosen to draw it around the Catholic and formerly Catholic countries of northern and central Europe, including, of course, those hotbeds of Christmas creepiness, Iceland and the British Isles. There will also be the odd excursion to North America, though only in relation to Old World practices preserved there. That said, no book of Christmas ghouls would be complete without the Greek *kallikantzaroi*, who slip uninvited down the chimney to cause havoc on Christmas Eve. Although they belong to the Eastern Orthodox realm, you will find them here, too, along with a handful of more northerly Christmas beasts (some naughty, others nice), the odd vampire, and a few unquiet child ghosts.

And what is Christmas without at least a sprig of something green? Now more than ever, Christmas is a hothouse holiday. Before the advent of the poinsettia, Christmas cactus, and overblown Yuletide cyclamen, humbler herbs had pride of place in the window, at the altar, and among the decorations in the hall. Along with the holly and the mistletoe, you will encounter some of the more unusual, sometimes haunted, seasonal greens, including ivy, juniper, and black hellebore.

Rest assured that there is more to see here than a few green wreaths, quaint witches, and prettily glowing ghosts. Few of the spirits you encounter will make your blood run cold, for the aim of this book is to capture the mystery of Christmas, not to evoke full-blown horror. Still, once you've read this book, you'll no longer dismiss that drumming on the rooftop as reindeer hooves. When you hear tinkling bells and a gruff "Ho *ho*," you'll be looking out for the Wild Hunt instead of Santa's sleigh, and as soon as you turn your calendar page to December, you'll be on the alert for the thump of a broom, the rustle of straw, or the brushing of birch twigs against the window pane.

Just as this continually evolving thing we call Christmas did not used to end on December 25, this book does not end at the Conclusion. At the back you will find a "Calendar of Christmas Spirits and Spells" to help you both organize and extend your festivities. There you will find the whole season at a glance as well as a few extra otherworldly tidbits not found elsewhere in the book. In the glossary I have defined terms not elucidated in the text. These range from familiar words whose exact meanings might nevertheless escape the reader, such as *distaff* and *flue*, to terms with which the reader may not be familiar at all, such as *primstav* and *Ember Days*. The glossary is also the receptacle of my less pertinent musings, which I have withheld from the main text in order not to break the flow.

CHAPTER ONE

A Thousand Years of Winter

If you speak English, then you are used to dedicating your Thursdays to the Germanic god Thor. Because the gnome-like *nisse* and *tomten* who watched over Nordic farmsteads refused to work on Thursday nights, we might jump to the conclusion that they were devotees of the thunder god. Thor's was always a popular cult, so it is possible that the wizened old fellows were his men, but first we should take a look at how the Norse, German, and Anglo-Saxon peoples reckoned their days. Just as all Jewish holidays begin at sundown before the day they are marked on the calendar, Germanic pagans counted their days from dusk to dusk instead of from daybreak to daybreak, which is why many if not most of the witches, ghosts, and goblins in this book fetch up in the darkness preceding each saint's feast day.

As soon as darkness has fallen on Thursday, "Thor's Day," we enter "Friday Eve," or, in the Germanic pagan imagination, Frigga's Eve. Frigga, who dwelt among the other sky gods in Asgard, was queen to Odin's king. She was a little less promiscuous than the fertility goddess Freya and decidedly more interested in housekeeping, especially the production of cloth. (This is not to say that Frigga and Freya were not two faces of the same goddess, which is also a distinct possibility.) Frigga was present in the northern sky in the form of her distaff, a constellation more familiar to us moderns as Orion's Belt. Spinning was forbidden on Frigga's Eve; an empty distaff next to a basket of full spools demonstrated to the goddess that you were a diligent sort and could afford, like the nisse and tomten, to slack off for one night. But by Twelfth Night (January 6), you had better have spun all the wool and flax in the house, for when the Christmas season was over, it would be time to set up the big upright loom, at which time you must have enough thread to warp it and start your weaving.

In Alpine lands, Frigga was known as Perchta, Berchta, or Bertha, and her cult continued to flourish long after the belief in goddesses had been swept under the straw. To make it clear that she no longer claims deity status, she now often goes by "Frau," meaning "Mrs." She has also been called *Spinnstubenfrau*, or "Spinning Room Lady." In Scandinavia, the icy twinkling of Frigga's distaff in the night sky was enough to keep the maids busy as bees, but elsewhere, young spinners had to be reminded that the last thing the goddess wanted to see when she peered in the window at Epiphany was a cloud of unspun wool or flax languishing on the distaff. In Germany, Austria, and Switzerland, there were numerous tales of Frau Berchta trampling and even setting fire to the half-spun fibers.

Though few of us do our own spinning these days, the last three Thursdays preceding Christmas still belong to Frau Berchta. She does not always put in an appearance on these "Berchtl Nights," as they are known in parts of the Alps; she has servants for that. Mostly, these servants make a racket. Bavarian children, appointing themselves temporarily to Frau Berchta's service, used to run around throwing dry peas, beans, and pebbles against the doors and windows to remind everyone that Christmas was coming. Because of the noise, these Thursdays were known in Germany as the "Knocking Nights." Homeowners rewarded the children for driving the evil spirits out from under the eaves. If the children happened to disturb any witches in the process, they did not fear pursuit, for the witch would be compelled to stop and count all of the beans that had fallen in her dooryard before she could go after the perpetrators.

The White Bees Are Swarming

In "The Snow Queen," when fat white snowflakes are swirling outside the window, the old grandmother tells little Kay and Gerda, "Those are the white bees swarming there!" Later, Kay spots the "queen bee" herself as she alights on the rim of an empty flowerpot as "a lady dressed in the finest white crape . . . composed of millions of starlike particles." Although there was no Frau Berchta afoot in Andersen's Denmark, the writer had traveled extensively through Europe, including the Alpine hinterlands where Berchta's larger servants still come to collect tribute for their Queen Bee, as they call her. Though the "queen" herself is nowhere in sight, her servants present themselves dutifully at the farmer's gate in grotesquely carved wooden masks. They remind the farmer that it is Frau Berchta who blankets the fields in snow so the soil can rest and yield generous crops next year. The farmer had better make an offering to these worker bees if he wants them to come back and dance in the fields at the close of winter and bless the furrows.

On Berchtl Nights, the goddess's Austrian servants take to the streets and create a din by ringing cowbells and playing tuneless music on their fiddles. These activities were not always confined to Advent Thursdays or to Austria. A fortnight before St. Andrew's Day (November 30) 1572, one Hans Buchmann claimed that he had been transported by supernatural agency from the forest near Rothenburg, Germany, to Milan, Italy. When he was first set upon, he thought he was under attack by a swarm of bees, but the buzzing then resolved itself into a terrifying scraping of bows on fiddle strings. We don't know what really happened to Hans—just before his disappearance he had borrowed some money without asking, so he had plenty of reason to fabricate the tale—but it is interesting that he should have thought to mention how the buzzing of bees had preceded his being lifted up and carried over the treetops. After that, he had to make his own way back to Rothenburg, finally arriving on Candlemas (February 2).

In the Alps of the same century, a visit from the *Salige Fräuleins* ("Blessed Young Ladies"), who came at night to sample food offerings left on the table, was announced by a softer bee-like music than the one Hans Buchmann heard. These Blessed Ones, as they are also called, would eventually make themselves over as the Christ Child's retinue and replace the humming with the tinkling of a tiny clapper bell. Still, wherever Berchta is remembered under her own name, we can expect to hear buzzing strings or at least some allusion to bees.

A Bird's-Eye View

Also running amok was Berchta's more northerly incarnation, Frau Holle, who used to take charge of all infants who died before they could be baptized. The stubbled fields over which the broomstick-mounted Frau Holle and her adopted children flew at Christmastime would be especially bountiful at the next harvest, but if you looked up at the flight of spirits as they passed overhead, you would be struck blind. Frau Holle eventually lost her sacred season in the north, but, thanks to the Brothers Grimm, she is remembered in fairy tale.

Frau Holle is the stereotypical German *Hausfrau.* The snow is the goose down that swirls into the sky when she shakes out her voluminous featherbed; the fog is the steam wafting up from the pots on her stove; and the thunder is the turning of her flax reel. Frau Holle was always looking for good help. To apply for the maid's position in her house, you first had to pass through water, either the pool in which she bathed to make herself young again, or an ordinary well.

In the Grimms' fairy tale "Frau Holle," an industrious though apparently clumsy girl drops her spindle down a well. Naturally, she goes in after it, emerging in a wonderful land full of flowers and sunshine. She wanders aimlessly, helping out a loaf of bread about to burn and a drooping apple tree along the way. Finally arriving at a cottage, she is greeted by a long-toothed old woman who introduces herself as Frau Holle and offers her a place in the household. The girl stays on to cook, clean, and help shake out the featherbeds, until she grows homesick. Frau Holle releases her without complaint, showering her with gold coins as she steps out the door.

Later, the girl's lazy stepsister dives down into the same well to see what *she* can get out of the old woman. She ignores both the imperiled loaf of bread and the apple tree, and when she gets to the cottage, she does little more than trail her fingers over the dusty furniture and swat half-heartedly at the bedclothes. When she announces that she is quitting, she gets a bucket of pitch dumped over her head.

While the German Frau Holle has been known to let herself go, her lack of youthful bloom is nothing compared to the horror that is Perchta. The Alpine Perchta is the image of Frau Holle as it might appear in that devilish, distorting mirror with which Andersen opens "The Snow Queen." The name Perchta dates back to the fourteenth century, while the first written reference to a horrible witch who presided over the winter festivities comes from Salzburg in the tenth. Who knows how long she might have been around before that? Of course, she may not always have gone by the name of Perchta; Jacob Grimm offers us the possibility that her name may have come from Old High German *giperahta naht*, or "shining night," that is, Epiphany (January 6), the night on which the Star shone down on Bethlehem. The fact that the old witch still has her own *Perchtentag*, or "Perchta's Day," on January 6, and that she is celebrated through all the Twelve Days of Christmas with the *Perchtenlauf*, or "Running of Perchta's servants," is a major accomplishment.

Yes, Perchta does have a pretty side, which is embodied by the "Pretty Perchten," who array themselves in flowery, cone-shaped headdresses, but most of her votaries appear as hairy, horned monsters, their huge mouths carved into grimaces. These "Evil Perchten" are not just ugly, but rowdy too. One of their jobs is to climb up on the village rooftops and drop snowballs down the chimneys.

How has Perchta managed to last so long? Certainly not by being pretty or nice. One of the secrets of her longevity may be her willingness to poke her long nose into other people's business, as we will see her doing on St. Barbara's and St. Lucy's Eve in chapter 9. Since the fifteenth century at least, Perchta has been portrayed with an inhumanly long nose. Sometimes described as "iron-nosed," her Austrian nickname, *Schnabelpercht*, "Beak Perchta," is more apt. Perchta was also supposed to have one splayed foot, ostensibly from pressing the treadle of her spinning wheel, but more likely to have been a goose or swan's foot. These avian vestiges, along with the white feathers that Frau Holle caused to fall from the sky, suggest that Perchta was used to assuming the shape of a bird, an ancient habit of Germanic goddesses like Frigga and Freya.

House Calls

Another strategy for holding on to power is to keep a close eye on one's subjects. Accordingly, the irrepressible old hag used to visit homes personally on the Eve of Epiphany

(January 5). If she liked what she found, the German Berchta might leave a gift of her own sky-spun yarn as a token of her approval. If this Yuletide goddess didn't like what she saw, then you had better beware. When she stepped over the threshold, she might be carrying a bundle of twigs, straw, or brushwood in one of her withered claws. Was she thinking of doing a little extra sweeping with that bundle of twigs? Or had she brought kindling for the fire? She might also be holding a brick, so perhaps she'd come to fix that chink in the garden wall? Unfortunately, it was none of the above.

Once she'd run her talon over the tops of the cupboards and counted the full spools of thread, the old biddy would want to know what you had made for supper and whether or not you remembered to put a little aside for her. She had better not smell any meat through that long beak of a nose, because the Eve of Epiphany meant a brief re-institution of the penitential fast that preceded Christmas. On this night, as the initials of the Three Kings were being chalked upon the lintel, the only permissible foods were fish and starch. Oatmeal with a little smoked herring on the side was one way to go, as was a thin pancake made of only flour and milk. Dumplings were a tastier solution. In the Thuringian forest of central Germany, Frau Holle was credited with the original potato dumpling recipe from which all others descend, while in Braunschweig to the north, she insisted only that no beans be eaten during the Twelve Days of Christmas.

But what if you forgot and went out for beer and sausages just before the old lady arrived? Or if you cooked the right dishes but forgot to leave an extra portion warming on the stove? The consequences would not be quite the same as if you had neglected to put out cookies for Santa, for Frau Berchta would be really, horribly upset. First, she would slit open your belly with the knife she kept hidden in her skirts. Then she would reach in and pull out all that forbidden food, replacing it with the bundle of kindling—or that brick—before she sewed you up again using farm implements instead of surgical instruments. She wouldn't do any of this right away but would wait until you were sleeping.

In the Icelandic *Laxdaela Saga*, An the Black, smith to Olaf Hoskuldsson, undergoes the same procedure not once but twice. In chapter 48, An dreams that a hag is standing over him with a meat cleaver and a wooden trough. Without a word, she cuts him open, scoops out his entrails, and stuffs him full of twigs. Was it something he ate? Scrooge might have said so, for did he not try to dismiss Marley's ghost as "an undigested bit of beef, a blot of mustard, a crumb of cheese, a fragment of underdone potato"? When An relates his experience at breakfast the next morning, the other men tease him, but his hostess interprets the vision as a warning.

Sure enough, in the next chapter, An and his traveling companions are engaged in a prolonged sword fight with the men of Laugar. By the time the fight is over, An's entrails are spilling out for real. He is presumed dead and laid out accordingly. But that night, he sits up suddenly in the candlelight, startling those who are keeping watch over his body. An assures them he was never really dead, only dreaming. The same strange woman had returned, extracted the load of kindling, and put his own bits back again. The smith makes a full recovery and is known as An Twig-belly forever after, or at least until chapter 55, when he gets his head split open while avenging the death of Kjartan Olafsson. Some wounds a witch just can't fix.

So if a knife-wielding Berchta appears to you on the heels of some overindulgence, know that she is not really stealing your gastrointestinal tract; she's just keeping it safe until you learn to make more intelligent choices.

The Lady of the Castle

In Switzerland, a "White Lady" who appears to be a glamorized version of the Spinnstubenfrau, and who was in fact known as "Bertha," was attached to a tenth-century castle tower on the shores of Lake Geneva. A White Lady is a tutelary spirit who takes it upon herself to guard treasures, announce impending deaths in a noble family, and even comfort the children. Each Christmas Eve, this Bertha materialized out of the fog dressed in a glowing white dress and carrying a scepter that at one time must have been a distaff, for she was especially interested in whether or not the girls had finished their spinning. In addition to inspecting the nearby households, she scattered handfuls of grain as she went. Like all queens, she never traveled alone but was trailed by an assortment of dwarves, kobolds, and other child-sized spirits as she set off from the foundations of her tower.

According to some accounts, this Bertha was the ghost of a historical queen, possibly a Swabian princess who married King Rudolph in the year 922. Others claim she was the mother or grandmother of Charlemagne. Whoever she might have been, the Swiss Bertha eventually outgrew her original identity. In time, she became even too big for the White Lady's boots, for her distaff and Yuletide appearance—not to mention that bird's foot she kept hidden inside the sparkling hem of her gown—all marked her as yet another incarnation of the queen of the gods.

All in all, this Bertha's haunting was of a very different sort from that carried out by another famous queen and Christmas ghost, Anne Boleyn, who used to appear in a white dress among the trees of the park outside her childhood home of Rochford Hall during the Twelve Days of Christmas. Because she had no special association with the later residents of Rochford Hall, except to terrify them, Anne cannot be counted as a proper White Lady. Besides, White Ladyhood requires a certain stick-to-itiveness that Anne's ghost lacked: during the same season in which she haunted Rochford in Essex, she was known to pop over, headless, to Hever Castle in Kent.

Falling midway between the ethereal Bertha and the earthbound Anne Boleyn is the most famous White Lady of all. For centuries, her ghost clung to a castle perched above the Vltava River, which also runs through Prague. While alive, she documented her existence so well that it is still possible to get to know her. She was born to the powerful House of Rožmberk (German Rosenberg) in southern Bohemia sometime in 1429. We don't know the exact date of her birth, but because she was christened "Perchta," it is tempting to think she might have been born or at least baptized during the Twelve Days of Christmas.

At the age of twenty, Perchta was given in wedlock to the recently widowed Jan of Lichtenstein. The union was a disappointment for them both. Much if not all of the conflict within the Lichtenstein home was precipitated by Perchta's father's nonpayment of the dowry. Far from helping matters was the presence of Jan's first wife's mother and sister, who treated the new wife like Cinderella. We know of Perchta's profound unhappiness from the many letters she wrote begging her father and brothers to come and rescue her or at least to send cash. In one of her portraits, Perchta is wearing a fine white dress but, tellingly, no jewels; she pawned the last of them in 1463 in a last-ditch effort to win her husband's affection. In 1465, she returned with her daughter to her old home at Český Krumlov Castle, her husband having forced her to leave their one surviving son behind. She never lived with Jan again, remaining with her brother's family until her death.

Compared to Anne Boleyn, Perchta slipped almost soundlessly into the afterlife, dying of the plague in 1476. Her mortal life became the palimpsest over which the story of her new career as White Lady was written, for her spirit stayed on at the old castle. Her ghost was described as a solemn lady in white holding a bunch of keys. She wore white gloves when she had good news to impart, black gloves when disaster loomed. Those who tried to speak to her as she glided along the passageways were rebuffed when she disappeared into the wall in a cloud of vapor. She was also known to make surprise inspections of the nursery, to the horror of the nursemaids. Perchta has kept a low profile since the death of the last Rožmberk, Petr Vok, in 1611, though she has been credited with tearing the Nazi flag from the castle's tower during World War II.

Within the castle at Český Krumlov is a Baroque, long-after-the-fact painting of Perchta in a white gown and loose blue sash, her hair in golden ringlets. She holds a slender rod with which she seems to be pointing to the sweep of arcane symbols inscribed at her feet. Whoever can decipher them, the legend says, will know where within the castle a great treasure is hidden. If you're going to try to decode Perchta's message yourself, I suggest you invoke the help of that other, older Perchta before her sacred season is over.

But be careful not to spend too much time on the puzzle; if you are meant to solve it, you will. Don't sit too long in the cold as Andersen's Kay did on the frozen lake in the middle of the Snow Queen's palace, arranging and rearranging the jagged shards of ice his mistress had given him. It was not until Gerda arrived and her tears dissolved the broken bit of mirror lodged in his heart that Kay was able, effortlessly, to spell out the word "Eternity." Washed out by his own tears, the tiny, silvered glass fragment in his eye, too, fell tinkling upon the ice.

In "The Snow Queen," the last we hear of the titular antiheroine is that she is going on holiday to whiten the vineyards and citron groves of the warm countries, but we know it is only a matter of time before she circles back to her blue-lit throne room north of the Arctic Circle. Old Perchta, too, will continue to make her rounds, carrying both winter and Christmas to all the lands through which she passes, for another key to long life is pride in one's work. Perchta's overriding mission has always been to serve as a grisly embodiment of winter, which can first be greeted with merry noise, then driven out again with as much, if not more, rejoicing.

"They say she ruled for a hundred years: a hundred years of winter," the Black Dwarf Nikabrik says admiringly of the White Witch in *Prince Caspian*. "There's power, if you like. There's something practical."

Craft: Distaff Tree

The word *distaff* means "fiber stick." Thus, the Old Norse *dísir* and Old English *idises*, tutelary spirits who presided over the birth of a child, determined the length, thickness, and overall quality of the thread that was to be that child's life*span*, just like the fairies in "Sleeping Beauty."

The most primitive kind of distaff is, indeed, a stick. It should be long enough that the spinner can hold it comfortably between her knees and have the cloud of unspun fibers at eye level, but not so long that she cannot tuck it under her arm if she wants to spin while walking. Any sapling or straight branch with an upward sweep of twigs on the end will do, such as ash, sycamore, or sassafras. No, you don't need a spindle; this distaff is for decorative purposes only.

In turn-of-the-last-century Pennsylvania, the poor city dweller's alternative to a fresh-cut Christmas tree was a branch of sassafras set upright in a stand, its branches covered in cotton batting. You don't have to use sassafras for this craft, but your branch or sapling should have the same upward sweep of twigs. Strip your branch of all leaves and any loose bits of bark. Wind each twig tightly around with a strip of cotton batting or unrolled cotton ball so it looks like the tree is covered in snow. Wrap the trunk or central branch as well. When your tree is all wrapped, adorn it with a short string of tiny lights. For a wintry look, I prefer clear or blue lights on a white wire. Set your creation in the window and call it a distaff, Christmas tree, or queen's scepter as you like. Because the cotton has not been spun, you will have to undress the twigs before the Spinnstubenfrau comes to inspect your work at Epiphany, but if you like, you can replace the lights on the bare twigs and keep them up until Candlemas.

Craft: White Witch Window Star

My little origami kitchen witch who flits around the house on a toothpick broomstick began life as the point of this star—hence the name of the following craft. To the trained eye, this star looks like a coven of eight white-cloaked witches gathered around a blossoming bonfire. To the untrained eye—your neighbor's, say—it's a simple winter decoration. Translucent paper window stars are a Christmas tradition in Germany and the Netherlands. The possible folding patterns are endless.

Tools and materials:

- Scissors
- Glue
- 2 sheets white origami paper 5⅞ inches square, each cut into quarters
- Clear tape

Take the first of your eight small squares of paper and fold it in half into a triangle. Fold in half again, then unfold all the way. You now have a cross to mark your center point (figure 1).

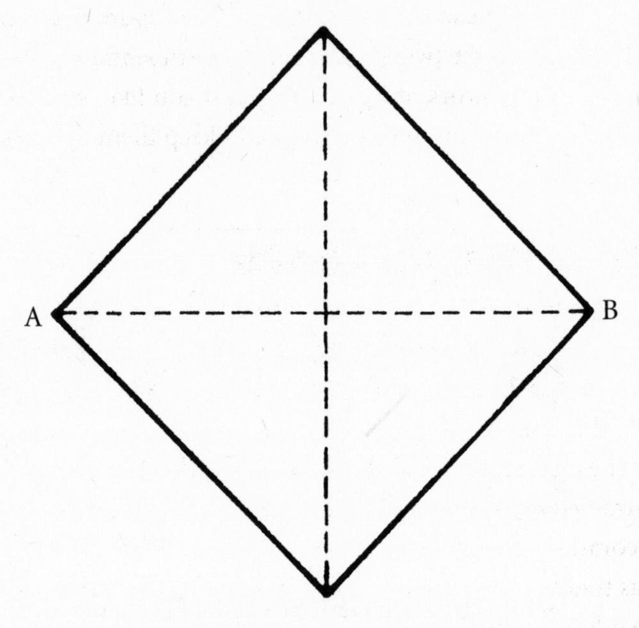

White witch window star, figure 1

Fold points A and B in to the center point as in figure 2.

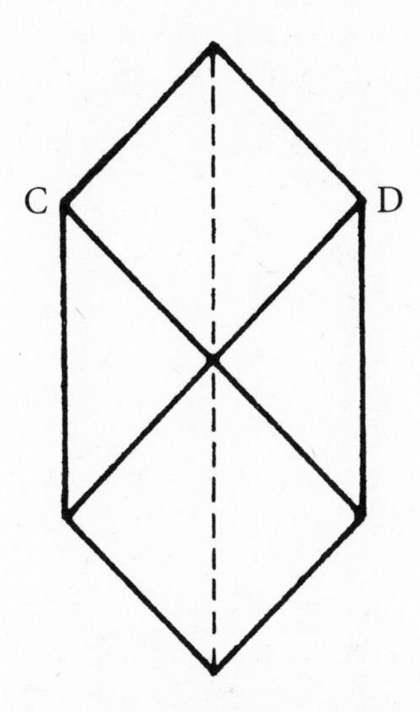

White witch window star, figure 2

Fold points C and D in to the center line. Here is your little witch, waiting to warm her hands at the fire (figure 3).

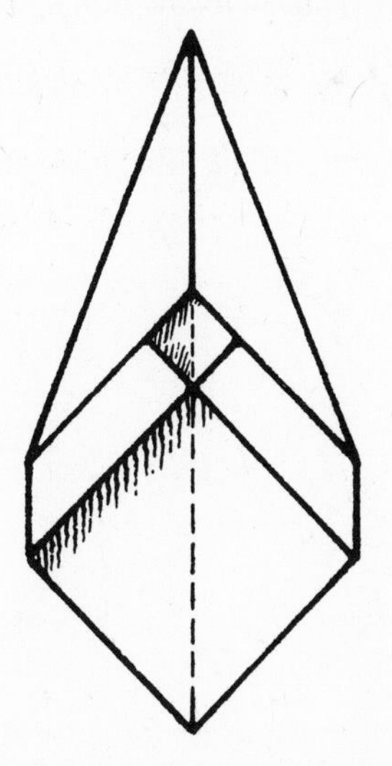

White witch window star, figure 3

Repeat all steps with the remaining seven squares of paper. Assemble by gluing each point (or "witch") half-overlapping the previous one (figure 4). A dab of glue is all you need.

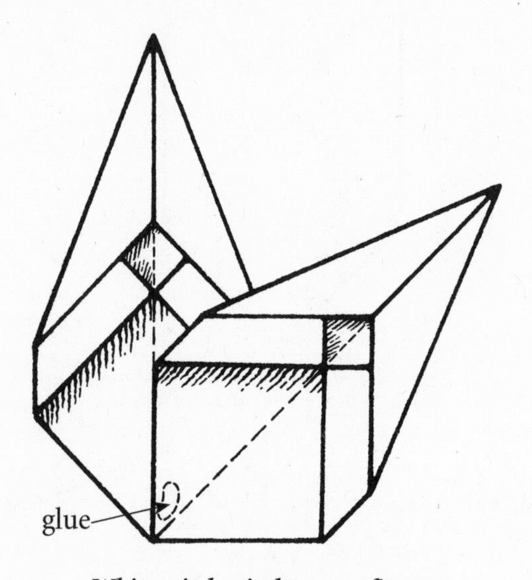

White witch window star, figure 4

When you have glued all the points (figure 5), and the glue is dry, press your star under a heavy grimoire for a day or two. Put a tiny roll of clear tape in the center of the star to stick it to the window.

White witch window star, figure 5

CHAPTER TWO

At Home with the Elves

Because the world of the elves is closely bound up with our own, it is in our own best interests to stay on the good side of these mysterious creatures. In the old days, this might mean the pouring of milk, blood, and even gifts of gold and silver into their earthen houses. Nowadays, it can be as simple as showing kindness and respect to a stranger, because you just never know. The elves in this chapter have no interest in making toys (or becoming dentists), nor are they particularly small. They have, however, always been a part of Christmas, even if their feast was originally held in October.

"What's with the Elves?"

We know that the feast of the elves was called *Álfablót,* or "Elf Sacrifice," and we know that it took place in southwestern Sweden, but we do not know exactly *what* took place. In fact, we know almost nothing about Álfablót, and that is the fault of a rather ill-tempered old farm wife who lived in the settlement of Hov in the year 1017. But before we take her to task, we must answer a question: who exactly are the elves?

"*Hvat er med alfom?*" or "What's with the elves?"[3] asks the prophetess in the Old Norse poem *Völuspá*. You may be asking the same question, for it is not yet December, and the battered rinds of the neighbors' jack-o'-lanterns are still moldering at the curb while the Thanksgiving turkey cools its heels in the freezer. *Hvat er med alfom?* indeed. The ancient Scandinavians regarded the *Álfar* as a distinct class of beings, though there was some fluidity among the bloodlines of elves, gods, norns, and even humans. Thirteenth-century Icelandic poet Snorri Sturluson offers us not one race of elves but two. Light elves, whom Sturluson likens to the sun, lived in Álfheim, or "elf home," which was located somewhere in the heavens. The dark elves, who were "blacker than pitch," dwelt deep inside the earth.

From earliest times, or the Bronze Age at least, elves were associated with the sun. In Sweden, cup-shaped depressions can be found in rocks bearing carvings of what we presume to be sun wheels. These stone cups held offerings of milk, which rural Swedes continued to pour out for the elves into the twentieth century. An Old Norse kenning for the sun itself is *álfröðull*, or "glory of the elves." The elves' role as

3. This line is more usually translated as "What of the elves?" but I prefer this one, provided by John Lindow under the entry "Elves," in his *Norse Mythology: A Guide to the Gods, Heroes, Rituals, and Beliefs*.

intermediaries between mortals and the life-giving sun helps to explain their shining aspect.

The highly literate Snorri Sturluson divided the elves neatly into light and dark, but this does not mean they were so divided throughout the Nordic world, or that every peasant who sought practical help from the elves was aware of such a division. The elves might have shone like the sun, but they were also very much of the earth. Because they were believed to be physically present in the landscape, they were often of more immediate importance to the farmer than were the mighty gods. It is possible that propitiation of the elves preceded worship of the gods, just as it has long outlived it in the general population, for the story of the elves does not end with Ragnarök, the fiery demise of the Old Norse worldview.

"Will You Know More?"

"*Vitod er enn?*" the *Völuspá* prophetess goes on to ask as she describes the end of that world. While many of the chieftains and kings of northern Europe were able to trade in Odin for Christ without much thought, the tillers of the soil had been working on their relationship with the elves for thousands of years and they were not about to give them up so easily. Rather than let the elves go, they resettled them within a Christian cosmology. In this new world, the elves were semi-fallen angels. When Lucifer rose up against God, the elves, or fairies, failed to choose sides and so they were not cast all the way down but were doomed to haunt the wild places of the earth until Judgment Day. The idea that these creatures of light reached their state because of the actions of the Angel of Light fit neatly with the old beliefs.

Another, rather more amusing theory has to do with an unexpected visit God paid to Adam and Eve long after they had been expelled from the Garden of Eden and set up house for themselves. By this time, they had so many children that Eve couldn't keep them all properly bathed, so she presented to God only the ones who had just come out of the tub. When God asked to see the rest of the children, Eve denied that there were any, having sent the filthy ones to hide in the backyard. (She had apparently not learned her lesson about lying to an omniscient deity.) God declared that those children whom Eve had hidden from him would remain hidden from all mankind. The descendants of these grubby children are the Hidden Folk, as they are known in Iceland to this day.

Of course, not everyone is satisfied with such apocryphal explanations. From the early to mid-twentieth century, it was fashionable to identify the elves and fairies as Europe's first settlers. In his 1955 book *Witchcraft Today*, original Wiccan Gerald Gardner equated them with the Picts and other tribes whose desire to keep the Old Ways in the face of Christianity sent them scurrying to the furthermost reaches of the Celtic realm, to the barren mountaintops and to dark holes in the hills where they could continue to practice their own brand of earthy magic. Already a small race compared to the Romano-Britons and Anglo-Saxons, their children were made smaller still by the deprivations of a life in hiding. These aboriginal "pixies," a corruption of "Picts" as Gardner would have it, kept very much to themselves, stealing out only at night to pinch butter, milk, and the occasional cow from their more agriculturally advanced neighbors. In between times, they occupied themselves with their ancient rituals and with making stone arrowheads tipped with poison, or "elf-shot."

What did these pixies look like? No doubt their hair was knotted into "elf locks" for want of a good combmaker, and at one time it was common knowledge that they were red-haired. In Washford Market, Somerset, they were also thought to be cross-eyed and to have "pointed ears, short faces, and turned-up noses."[4] The observation that redheads could pop up unpredictably in otherwise blond or dark-haired families may have had to do with this belief. Rather than attribute such children's coloring to a recessive gene or to the milkman, parents might regard them as changelings—the cast-off progeny of the pixies.

We know from the Romans that the Picts brushed themselves with a blue paint that may have been mineral-derived, though the more popular explanation is that it was derived from indigo extracted from the woad plant (*Isatis tinctoria*).[5] According to Gardner, when they wanted to go unnoticed, they mixed this blue colorant with a dye made from the yellow-flowered weld (*Reseda luteola*), the result

4. Quite often, the terms *fairy*, *elf*, and *pixy* are used interchangeably. However, as Ruth L. Tongue explains in *Somerset Folklore*, the Somerset pixies defeated the fairies at some mythical point in time and drove them all west of the River Parrett. Since we mortals are not all of one tribe, it should come as no surprise that our otherworldly neighbors have also divided themselves into factions.
5. The writers who described these blue warriors did not make it clear if their skin was only painted or tattooed. If the latter were the case, an ink made from woad would have been the sensible choice since woad reduces swelling when applied to the skin.

being a whole race of tiny men and women roaming the moors in varying shades of blue and Lincoln green, the latter eventually becoming the national color of Faerie.

Like their Neolithic ancestors, these beleaguered but colorful "little people" maintained homes of dry-stone construction half sunk in the earth; perhaps even elaborate complexes of them as can be seen at Skara Brae in the far north of Scotland. Since the whole house was covered in grass or heather, it would have looked to the casual eye like a natural feature of the landscape. If one of the "big people" happened to be passing by on a winter's night and witness the opening of a well-concealed door, he could not have failed to notice the blaze of hearth light staining the snow as it does at the doors of elvish abodes in so many folktales of northwestern Europe. There would have to have been smoke holes in those hollow hills through which the scents of the bracken fire and roasted shrew could have escaped, but these details are seldom present in the folklore. Gardner insists that most of the coming and going would have been through those primitive chimneys, which only added to the pixies' exoticism in the eyes of their neighbors.

Unfortunately, this Gardnerian version of elvish origins probably has a lot more romance in it than truth. Instead, Gardner's concept of the "mighty dead" might give us a better idea of who the elves really are. The mighty dead are the spirits of magical practitioners—"witches," if you will—who, through a series of reincarnations, have honed their skills to the point where they, in death, have become objects of worship or at least consultation.

The elves were certainly revered, but one would hesitate to call them mighty. Especially in the Scandinavian folktales that were first recorded in the nineteenth century by roving ethnographers inspired by the Brothers Grimm, the elves appear to carry on lives that parallel those of their human neighbors. They move their cattle from one pasture to another and spread their hay to dry in the sun. They cook, clean, and concern themselves with the welfare of their children. They even attend their own church services, though they appear not to have undergone either Reformation or Counter-Reformation, even in those countries where the humans were staunchly Protestant. Often, the elves are possessed of an unearthly beauty, but just as often they appear as ordinary people, albeit in quaint dress.

If the elves resemble us, it is because they *are* us, or, rather, they *were*. The human who stumbles upon a procession of elves or an impromptu elvish feast is often startled to recognize someone he knows among them: someone who has died either recently or years before. Often, this dead acquaintance advises the human witness how to safely leave the party, the standard precaution being not to touch the food. The elves, then, are the dead—not the quietly resting dead but those who, for whatever reason, have taken up new lives on the other side of the veil and at times, either knowingly or unknowingly, might come strolling back through it.

Among these elves are the long-dead who speak a language the barest traces of which are remembered in the names of hillocks that used to be mountains, or of rivers that have long ago changed course. The bones of these people have become fully incorporated into the soil, yet still they rattle about the landscape on their elvish business. They no longer remember any other kind of existence and may be only dimly aware of developments since their passing. They are troubled by the tolling of church bells and might be scalded by the dripping of holy water into their homes, not to mention the seeping of car exhaust, for these things belong to a world they no longer do.

The more recently dead, in their petticoats and high-crowned hats, have crossed over just long enough ago not to notice anything strange about the banquet, how the candles blaze but never burn down, how the platters of cakes are never diminished. But the sweetheart who was put in the churchyard just last week has not yet been fully absorbed into the company of elves. She can still remember who belongs on which side of the divide and will do what she can to prevent her living loved ones from being taken up prematurely by the dead.

An Offering to the Elves

It is time now to join Sigvat[6] the Scald, or court poet, on a journey he has undertaken through southwestern Sweden on behalf of the Norwegian King Olav. It is the "beginning of winter." Since this is the Viking Age, in which the year was divided into a summer and a winter half, this puts us somewhere around the time of our Halloween. No doubt

6. "Sigvat" is the spelling used in Erling Monsen and A. H. Smith's translation of Snorri Sturluson's *Heimskringla: or, Lives of the Norse Kings*. If you are looking for the scald in another translation, you might find him under "Sighvat." The episode concerned takes place in chapter 91 of *The History of St. Olav* in *Heimskringla*.

snow has already fallen on the forest of Eidaskog, though the river is not yet frozen. Sigvat and his small party of king's men are cold, footsore, and probably hungry to boot. Darkness is falling as they emerge from the woods at Hov. In search of beds or at least a pile of straw for the night, they approach the first farm they see, but the door is barred. As Sigvat attempts to stick his nose in the crack, it is explained to him by those within that he has arrived at a holy time, that the space inside is already consecrated and he may not enter. Since this is no church but a farmhouse, Sigvat, an Icelandic Christian, assumes correctly that it is a heathen observance. He curses the farmer, either for his lack of hospitality or his backward ways or both, and goes on his way.

Scald and king's men continue to the next farmyard, where they are again turned away, this time by an old woman who calls Sigvat a "wretch" and informs him that "they are holding an offering to the elves." Her use of the third person suggests she may be a servant sent by the family to get rid of the unwanted visitors. We can only wish she had opened the door, for the compulsive versifier Sigvat would surely have left us a detailed, if biased, description of the ceremony had he been allowed inside to witness it. As it is, we can only wonder. How was the family dressed? In workaday clothes or in special garments reserved for the occasion? Did lights burn within? How was the table laid, or was all the action going on in the enclosed courtyard?

We cannot lay all of the blame at the feet of the "old hag," as Sigvat calls her, for Sigvat's behavior is just as intolerable. Though an Icelander and a Christian, Sigvat is presumably of Norwegian descent. He should therefore have been familiar with the *Dísablót*, or "sacrifice to the *dísir*," which his own heathen grandparents and possibly even parents would have celebrated at "winter-nights" at the same time of year. The Dísablót took place before an altar dedicated to the dísir, ancestral female spirits who are the precursors of our fairy godmothers and a few of our witches, too.

There is a lot of overlap between the dísir and the norns who sat spinning among the roots of the World Tree. Like the dísir, the norns occasionally made house calls but all in all were considered to be more aloof than the dísir. Sometimes the dísir behaved more like bloodthirsty valkyries than fairy godmothers, and, in fact, the Dísablót altar was reddened with blood, though we are not sure whose. In the *Saga of Hervor and King Heidrek*, the Dísablót is presided over by one Princess Álfhild of Álfheim, so it is possible that the Álfablót and Dísablót were precisely the same thing. Had Sigvat shown a little respect for the traditions of Hov, he might have been allowed to slip quietly inside and take part in the feast.

He might even have been asked to play his harp, if harp he had, and if his fingers were not too stiff with cold, for it was not unheard of for a Christian to join in heathen rituals in times of need. In the *Saga of Erik the Red*, Sigvat's fellow Icelander, Gudrid, now a Christian, is persuaded to assist the prophetess Thorbjorg by chanting the magical formulae she had learned as a child. Unfortunately, there was no such syncretism that evening in Hov, and Sigvat is turned away by four more bonders before he gives up his search for hospitality. When he finally arrives at his ultimate destination, the hall of Ragnvald the Jarl, he is rewarded with a gold ring and sympathy, so you really can't feel sorry for Sigvat.

Was the Álfablót unique to that district of Sweden? The only other reference we have to a sacrifice made to the elves occurs in *Kormak's Saga*. Here, a witch directs the wounded Thorvald to invoke the healing power of the elves by pouring bull's blood on a nearby elf mound and making a feast of the meat for the elves dwelling within. Could the Hovians have been sacrificing something more precious than livestock? Human sacrifice was certainly not unknown at this time in this part of the world, but had that been the case, then surely the farm folk would have dissembled in front of the Christian Sigvat, pleading sickness in the house rather than announcing the occasion of a sacrifice. And whereas a portion of the livestock had to be slaughtered at the onset of winter anyway, humans were valuable members of the workforce and not to be dispatched lightly.

So why the secrecy? The celebrants may have been in the process of inducing a trance state in one or more of the family members or even of a visiting prophetess like Thorbjorg. The speaking of prophecies serves as the highlight of several feasts in the Old Norse sagas. Much work went into preparing both the speaker and the space, so if this were the case, it is no wonder the old woman was short with Sigvat. She would have been eager to learn what the future held for her and therefore anxious not to break the spells that had been woven about the scrying platform.

Ironically, the man who sent Sigvat on his errand in the first place, the Christian King Olav, was in some respects an elf himself. Though Olav denied even the possibility, a few of his followers believed him to be the reincarnation of an earlier king, Olav Geirstader, who, upon his death and laying "in howe" (i.e., in his grave mound), received both offerings and the epithet of *álf*, or "elf," after his name. It is also interesting to note that Hov lay just to the east of the limits of a kingdom still known in the early Middle Ages as Álfheim. Scholars argue that the name has nothing to do with elves but refers instead to the bed of gravel that lies beneath the tillable soil of this district, a fact that Tolkien fans will quickly forget when they hear that, in the ninth century, Álfheim was ruled by a king named Gandálf. According to one of the *Fornaldar Sagas*, or "Sagas of Ancient Days," the inhabitants of this earthly Álfheim were so fair of face that only the *risir* outshone them. As to who the risir were, I suppose that is another story.

Like Christmas Itself

You probably have to clean house before Thanksgiving anyway, so why not host your own Álfablót this year? (Elves, like most Christmas spirits, love a clean house.) As witnessed at Hov, the door need not be opened to anyone outside the family—anyone living, that is—so you won't have to do much shopping or decorating. Now, the question to ask is: How would the elves wish to be fêted?

If you are already following a Norse or Saxon Pagan path, you may be able to commune with the elves and ask them yourself. The rest of us must turn to the old tales for clues. One of the most helpful is the Norwegian fairy tale "The Finn King's Daughter." Here we have a Finnish princess playing the starring role in a Norwegian story whose roots have been traced back to Jutland in Denmark, a pan-Scandinavian folktale if ever there was one.[7] All that's missing is the Swedish element, but I say the Swedes missed the chance to put in their two *kronor* when they shut the door in Sigvat's face back in 1017.

Although she is not identified as an elf in the tale as it was collected by Rikard Berge in 1900, the Finn King's daughter bears such a close resemblance to the Álfar that she must once have been one. Here are the bare bones of the story:

Before going off to war, the Finn King encloses his beloved daughter inside a mound, mostly because he's caught her exchanging glances with the new serving boy. When the princess and her nine handmaidens are well and truly shut up in their well-appointed house of earth, the king departs, never to return. The princess and her maids begin at once to try to dig their way out. The effort takes nine years and the life of each of her maids. At last, the princess claws her way out into the now unfamiliar countryside. While she is rambling round the forest, lost, the king's men finally return to the mound to release her, the Finn King himself having died of sickness. They find nothing except, presumably, the bones of her handmaidens.

After a search of the kingdom turns up no princess, a troll woman presents herself at the Finn King's hall and claims to be the missing girl. She immediately starts planning her wedding to the serving boy, who, by this time, has revealed

7. "The Finn King's Daughter" is an example of what is known to folklorists as Tale Type 870: The Princess Confined in the Mound, and is found outside Scandinavia as well. See Reidar Christiansen's book *Folktales of Norway*.

himself as an exiled prince—of course!—and, having earlier earned the Finn King's deathbed blessing, has taken up residence in the hall. He goes along with the wedding plans (People change, don't they? And this girl had been in a *mound* for nine years!), but he is clearly not looking forward to the upcoming nuptials.

At last, the real princess emerges from the forest, chilblained and emaciated. Rather than declare her true identity, she takes a job as a maid at her old home and helps the troll woman to pass a series of tests by which the prince is hoping to expose her as an impostor. We are not told why the real princess lets it drag on for so long, but eventually the troll woman is tripped up by an incident involving a pair of gloves, and the Finn King's daughter takes her proper place at the prince's side.

Those are the bare bones; the elvishness emerges in the details of the story. Unlike the trollish impostor who can barely thread a needle, our plucky princess is a whiz at sewing and the textile arts, both elvish traits in nineteenth-century folklore—think of "Rumpelstiltskin" and "The Shoemaker and the Elves." She's also good with the horses, like the Scandinavian household sprites who mucked out the stables and braided the horses' manes.

Elves were believed to dwell in mounds, and it was to these mounds that mortals went to offer sacrifice. In the opening of "The Finn King's Daughter," the father stocks the mound with "food and drink, clothing and cups and vessels." The poor girls are going to need all these things, of course, but these are also exactly the sorts of gifts that were laid with the dead in howe in pagan days. (Celtic fairies and brownies were highly offended by gifts of clothing, but their Nordic counterparts expected them.) Other than these basic provisions, the Finn King does not take into account any practical considerations such as a conduit for fresh air or waste disposal system. And would it not have been simpler and far more humane for him to have appointed a guardian to look after his daughter in his absence? Could he not have sent her to stay with relatives or at the very least have banished the serving boy? The answer is no, because practical considerations are for the living, and as soon as she enters the mound, the princess enters the elvish realm: the realm of the dead.

So there they are, the princess and her nine doomed handmaidens, without door or smoke hole such as Gardner's euhemeristic pixies enjoyed. They blink at one another in panic as, within, the candlelight glances off the silver cups and plates and, without, the last shovelfuls of clay are tamped down above their heads. Those nine years inside the mound must have seemed like a lifetime to the princess, and when she finally scrabbles her way out, it really does seem like a lifetime or more has passed. Even before he departed, the Finn King had ordered the mound leveled—suggesting that the "living" space was very deep inside the earth—and sown over with grass. By the time the princess breaks out, the forest has taken over the razed site, obliterating all familiar features of the landscape. Like Rip Van Winkle, she recognizes no one at her old home, with the exception of the former serving boy, and no one recognizes her. Our princess is not simply a lost daughter; she is one of the mighty dead, coming home to a world much changed. Toward the end of the tale, she and her prince enjoy a church wedding, so it is obviously a Christian world to which she has returned. Originally, she would have been a heathen princess, most likely also a priestess, buried along with a sacred number of her servants and the finest of her worldly goods and ritual paraphernalia.

But where was our princess all that time the Finn King's men were scouring the forest for her? It turns out she was attending a sort of Álfablót. Devastated and disoriented, she is taken in for a time by a party of charcoal burners. This is the first human company she has had since her last handmaiden died. The charcoal burners offer her a bed inside their leafy shelter, a bowl of rabbit stew, and a seat close by the fire. The story tells us, "It seemed like Christmas itself to her after what she had been through."[8] What did they talk about there in the firelight? Conversation would not have been easy, for the princess's courtly speech was probably no more closely related to the deep woodsmen's jargon than the language of the light elves was to that of the dark elves. What mattered was the treatment she received.

Heat, light, food, and a human welcome: keep these in mind if you want to host the Álfar. Schedule your "Christmas for the Elves" somewhere in that empty stretch of time between Halloween and Martinmas (November 11), or even between Martinmas and Thanksgiving, so they won't have to share their special day. The elves are bearers of light, so if you cannot manage a full moon for your feast, a waxing crescent

8. Had it actually been Christmas, the charcoal burners would not have been in the forest to meet her, for charcoal burning was done only during the windless days of summer.

is better than a waning three-quarter moon. Just as the princess had to claw her way out of the earth, wander the forest barefoot, and cross a river on the back of a wolf, your guests will have completed a long and arduous journey. They have left their usual haunts and howes in order to join you, so greet them warmly. I suggest the following: "Let them come who wish to come, and let them go who wish to go, and do no harm to me or mine."[9] Once you have issued this invitation, I would advise you not to address the elves directly.

You don't know how far some of them may have come in space or time, so it's a good idea to turn off the television and most electric lights, which the oldest of the company may find glaring. If you have a fireplace, make a fire. Otherwise, light plenty of candles. Set the table with your best dishes but offer simple foods: bread, meat, milk. If you are very lucky, you will get some dísir along with the Álfar. These ladies may be expecting a reddened altar, so now would be the time to bring out that blood-red Christmas tablecloth or runner. Feel free to talk and laugh with any living company—it's a party, after all—but keep in mind that it is all done in honor of the elves. Don't be a Hovian; leave the door ajar for the duration of the feast, and don't be surprised if you see a few familiar faces shining out from the shadows.

9. These words are spoken by the Cinderella figure in "The Sisters and the Elves," on page 55 of Jacqueline Simpson's book *Icelandic Folktales and Legends*. In the West Fjords of Iceland, it was customary to speak such formulae at either Christmas or New Year's Eve.

Craft: Elvish Window Ornament

Because we know so little about it, Álfablót is a feast that is open to interpretation. If you've already hosted the dead at Halloween, you may choose this occasion to celebrate the solar aspect of the light elves. The following craft is meant to be displayed in the window, where it will filter the light of the sun.

Tools and materials:

2 flimsy, plain white paper plates
Plain white paper, the thinner the better
Colored pencils and/or markers
Glue
Scissors
X-Acto or other craft knife
String

Cut out the centers of both your paper plates. Trace one of these cut-out circles on your plain white paper. Draw the face of the sun or moon inside the circle and color it in. Cut out the face, leaving a quarter-inch margin all around. Glue the face into the empty center of one of your plates with the colored side on the convex side of the plate.

Glue a knotted loop of string to the inside edge of one of the plates. Glue the two plates together, concave side to concave side, then decorate the fluted rim on each side.

In the daytime when the sun is shining in, turn your ornament so that the colored side faces out. The incoming sunlight will illuminate the celestial face. When the lights are on inside, turn the colored side in.

Elvish window ornament

CHAPTER THREE

Dead by Christmas Morning

We have not quite finished with the elves, which is just as well since, with the television off, you'll need a few more stories to keep your guests entertained at Álfablót. We've already learned something about the nature of our friends from the other side of the veil as well as how to entertain them. In this chapter we'll examine the more sinister implications of opening your home to the elves.

Queen of the Elves

For years, Hild, a middle-aged housekeeper on a sheep farm tucked somewhere in the green mountains of Iceland, had graciously volunteered to stay at home and prepare the feast while the rest of the household attended church on Christmas Eve. This should have been the first clue that the housekeeper was not what she seemed, but somehow it just didn't click with the widowed farmer who employed her. You see, in medieval Iceland, no one in his or her right mind would offer to stay home alone on the most dangerous night of the year.

The "Dead by Christmas Morning" motif is a tradition that certainly predates both the Old Norse sagas and Christmas itself.[10] In the old Icelandic stories, death was not the inevitable outcome for the unfortunate servant left to himself or herself on Christmas Eve, but it was a very real possibility. If she was lucky, she might only be driven mad or carried off into the mountains, never to be seen again.

Hild, on the other hand, lives to see the dawn each Christmas morning and is never any the worse for it. In fact, she shows every sign of having been busy the whole night through: the floors are swept, the tapestries hung, and there is the butter, *skyr*, smoked mutton, and a box of snowflake breads all ready to be eaten by the hungry churchgoers when they return. Unfortunately, a succession of newly hired shepherds has not fared so well.

If the farm were not so remote, as Icelandic sheep farms tend to be, the master would take all his hands to church with him. But the church is a long way off and the household must set out early in order to make it in time for the Midnight Mass. As for the sheep, they never take a day off; so as long as there are a few patches of grass peeking out from the ice and snow, they must be taken out to graze, then returned at nightfall to the comfort of the fold. So,

10. The tradition lives on in Otfried Preussler's 1971 children's novel *Krabat*, though in *Krabat* it is on New Year's morning that the journeyman's corpse is found at the bottom of the stairs. *Krabat* has been translated into English as *The Satanic Mill*, which has to be the reason why it has never become a holiday standard in the English-speaking world.

while the farmhouse remains in Hild's competent care, one of the shepherds—and it's always the new guy—must stay behind to look after the sheep.

And each Christmas morning, the farmer has returned to find the lone shepherd dead in his bed. Since there is never so much as a mark on the poor fellow, the farmer really cannot guess the cause. Hild would seem the obvious suspect, but surely she was too busy polishing the candlesticks and making pretty patterns in the butter to have murdered anyone. And what motive would she have had for wishing all of those shepherds dead?

After having buried several young men in his employ, the farmer decides he will take on no new hands; he'll stay behind with the sheep himself if he has to. But that summer, a young tough arrives at the farm and applies for a job. He must be some kind of desperado, for he seems eager to work there despite the rumors he's heard. The farmer is reluctant to take him on, but the young man is insistent, and, sure enough, he stays to take charge of the sheep on Christmas Eve.

The tale does not include any awkward encounters between shepherd and housekeeper over the course of the day. If the place is anything like the historic Glambaer farm in Skagafjord in the north of the country, then this is not surprising. Icelandic farmhouses are sprawling affairs, and the shepherd's work would have kept him some distance from it. Returning at night to the *baðstofa*, or main living quarters, he would have eaten his supper sitting on his bed while Hild was still busy in the kitchen.

Wearily, the shepherd wipes his bowl and spoon with a wisp of straw, stows his dishes, and tucks himself into bed. He fights sleep, but it's an uphill battle, and his eyes are just sliding closed when he hears the housekeeper enter the baðstofa. Now only feigning sleep, he allows her to fix a bridle about his head. He does not fight her as she tugs at the headstall and leads him out under the cold stars. She climbs on his back and proceeds to ride him at great speed deep into the mountains.

It would make a less ridiculous picture if Hild had used the bridle to turn the shepherd into one of those adorably shaggy Icelandic horses, but this is not the case. Her mount is still a man, and her magical instrument is the *gandreiðarbeizli*[11] or "elf-ride bridle," more commonly translated as "witch's bridle." Made from the bones and skin of a recently buried corpse, it allowed the witch to turn any creature or object into a swift, convenient means of transport. It might have been kinder for Hild to have used a milking stool, butter churn, or brewing vat to get where she was going, but then we would have no story.

And before we judge the housekeeper too harshly, it must be mentioned that detailed instructions for making the so-called witch's bridle date only to the seventeenth century, when the Icelanders, like their continental counterparts, had become obsessed with witches of the Satanic sort and with a malevolent magic grounded in the freshly turned earth of the graveyard. While the practices of the early modern era could be downright disgusting, the gandreiðarbeizli is actually an

11. Yes, *gand* as in "Gandalf." *Gand* is a word of uncertain meaning, but it has retained its undeniably magical overtones.

artifact of the ancient gandreið, the Elf-Ride or Wild Hunt. While the passing of the gandreið was always an ominous occurrence, its heathen witnesses were usually more awestruck than horrified. In *Njal's Saga*, chapter 125, the Norse god Odin appears as a black figure on a gray horse inside a ring of flames. The horse is described as a creature of both ice and fire, while the rider uses his torch to ignite the sky above the eastern mountains. Could this be the aurora borealis? The post-saga storytellers of Borgarfjörður tell us that the gandreiðarbeizli made a whistling, rattling sound, as the northern lights are sometimes said to do.

But our housekeeper on her human mount has now come to a deep and faintly glowing fissure among the rocks. Without hesitation, she dismounts and clambers down into it, soon disappearing from sight. What is our shepherd to do? Though still in human form, the magic has robbed him of the use of his hands, so he must rub his head against a boulder to free himself from both the bridle and the enchantment. There must be more to this young stranger than meets the eye, for he happens to be carrying a magic stone in his pocket, and as soon as the bridle is off, he takes the stone in his left palm, immediately blinking out of sight. Invisible, he follows Hild in among the rocks.

Once through the fissure, we are not in Iceland anymore. On the other side, the terrain is much smoother. We are given little description of Elfland, but one would guess that there is no snow here and that the plain is bathed in a golden twilight, for, despite the late hour, the shepherd has no trouble making out the shape of the housekeeper or of the great, gilded hall toward which she is bound. Once inside its doors, Hild exchanges her housekeeper's apron for a queen's regalia and, gathering her rich skirts in her hands, settles herself in the high seat beside the King of Elfland. There she is attended by her five children as well as a whole host of courtiers. The elves, who appear quite human, are all dressed to the nines, and the long trestles are laid for a feast. In one corner, however, the shepherd notices an old lady sitting apart from the glittering throng, hands folded, sour-faced and radiating the dark aura of a malevolent fairy.

Queen Hild dandles her children and converses with her husband. The royal elf family appears at once both happy and inconsolable. The shepherd observes the bittersweet tableau, at the same time taking care not to tread on any of the dancing courtiers' toes. Meanwhile, the queen has given one of her gold rings to her youngest child to play with. When the child drops it on the floor, the shepherd swoops down, snatches the ring, and slips it on his own invisible finger.

As we know it must, the hour arrives for Queen Hild to depart. She rises, puts off her queenly robes, and knots her kerchief over her hair. Her husband and children are weeping and tearing at their elfin locks, but what can she do? She is doomed to return to the mortal realm. The elf king appeals to the grim figure in the corner, but if help is to be had from that quarter, the old lady will not give it. As Queen Hild bids them all a tearful farewell, the shepherd creeps out of the hall ahead of her, hurrying back across the plains of Elfland, scrambling up and out of the gap in the rocks just in the nick of time. When Hild climbs up after him, he has pocketed both the gold ring and the invisibility stone, replaced the magic bridle about his head, and assumed a vacant stare. The erstwhile queen mounts him, none the wiser, and home they go.

Christmas morning on the farm is a happy one for a change, for the new shepherd is found alive in his bed. He tells the farmer of the odd "dream" he has had and of the part the enigmatic housekeeper played in it. Hild denies everything . . . unless he can produce some evidence of his adventure? At this, the shepherd produces the little ring of elf-gold.

At the sight of it, Hild sighs and confides that hers is a rags-to-riches story. In Elfland, she had been no more than a lowly servant, but the Elf King fell in love with her nevertheless. His mother disapproved of the match. Though an elf herself, Hild was placed under an *álög*, or elf-uttered curse—in this case, one uttered by her mother-in-law. Banished from the royal residence and from Elfland itself, Hild was compelled to ride a man to death each Christmas until such time as she was found out and executed as a witch. That had been her mother-in-law's plan, but this year's man lived to tell the tale. Because he'd had the courage to follow her along the Lower Road, he had freed her from the álög. (It is not clear why his time in harness had not killed him, for Hild got just as much mileage out of him as she had from the others. It may be that not falling asleep was the key.) Having related all this, Queen Hild has no further need of the witch's bridle to reach her home; she simply vanishes.

Our shepherd, we are told, eventually married and took up farming for himself. He did so well that folk credited his prosperity to the beneficence of the Queen of the Elves.[12] As for the farmer, with the curse now lifted, we can assume he had no more trouble getting good help.

Recipe: Icelandic Snowflake Breads

In Iceland, the beginning of the Christmas season means it's time to make *laufabraud*, snowflake breads. If you're worried that the trolls might eat up all your hard work, you can hide your pastry snowflakes in a tin in the garage until Christmas Eve. The "breads" in this recipe are smaller than traditional examples—which are eight to nine inches in diameter—so they can be fried in a smaller pan.

Ingredients:

- 1¾ cups flour
- 1 teaspoon baking powder
- 1 teaspoon sugar
- 1 Tablespoon unsalted butter
- 1 cup whole milk
- Lard
- Powdered sugar

In a large bowl, sift flour, baking powder, and sugar together. Set aside.

Heat milk and butter until butter is melted. Do not boil. Add milk and butter to flour mixture a little at a time, stirring, then working with your hands until you have a stiff dough. Add more flour if needed.

12. "Hild, Queen of the Elves," along with accompanying notes, can be found on pages 43–52 of Jacqueline Simpson's *Icelandic Folktales and Legends*. See same, page 180, for detailed instructions for making a witch's bridle, if you must.

Icelandic snowflake breads

Knead dough on lightly floured surface until you can form it into a smooth ball. Divide the ball into thirty-two equal parts and form each part into a smooth, round ball. Cover balls with a damp cloth.

On a floured surface, roll each ball out with a rolling pin to about ⅛-inch thickness or about 5 inches in diameter. Try to keep them nice and round. Stack rolled-out rounds between sheets of waxed paper.

Heat about 1½ inches of lard in a frying pan. While it's heating, you can make your snowflakes. You can prick patterns directly into the round with the point of a sharp knife or, making sure it is well-floured, fold the round into quarters and snip the pattern in with scissors just as you would make a paper snowflake. You can cut little triangles out of the dough or cut triangular flaps and press them back.

When the lard is hot enough to make a droplet of water hiss and spit, lay the first snowflake gently in it. Fry each side for about 30 seconds or until golden brown.

Drain snowflakes on paper towels and sprinkle with powdered sugar when cool.

Home but Not Alone

In "Hild, Queen of the Elves," the hero must travel to Elfland, but it is actually more common for the elves to invite themselves onto the farm. This folktale motif is known as "The Christmas Visitors." Most often it is a young girl who is left home but not quite alone. One Icelandic version comes to us from the pen of the rather schoolmarmish Hólmfrídur Árnadóttir, whose childhood memoir, *When I Was a Girl in Iceland*, was one of a series published in the early 1900s.

Árnadóttir writes of a "young maiden," the new girl, left behind for unspecified reasons on Christmas Eve. Not as industrious as Hild, she lights the candles in the baðstofa and settles down to read the Bible. The fact that she has a Bible and knows how to read it tells us that we have now entered the Protestant era in Iceland. The story could even be taking place in Hólmfrídur's own day, by which time not much else had changed since the Viking age except for the introduction of the spinning wheel and coffee mill.

The heroine is concentrating on the printed words before her when who should come trooping into the room but a "crowd" of people of all ages. There is nothing sinister about them; in fact, they're in a festive mood and eager for the pious maid to join in their dancing, but she ignores them and continues reading. The dancers offer her "beautiful presents," but the imperturbable girl does not even look up from her book. The party goes on all night without her giving in to temptation, though she must have had to pull her feet up on the bed to let the swirling couples by. No ballroom to begin with, the baðstofa would have been crowded with chairs, spinning wheels, and beds—the one at Glambaer contained eleven—so there would not have been room to swing a Yule Cat (see chapter 8), let alone host a dance.

Hólmfrídur gives no indication that the uninvited guests are diminutive or even that they are elves, but they are certainly no ordinary neighbors, for at dawn they vanish, leaving the baðstofa just as it was. It would be nice to hear that they left a few gifts behind to pay for the use of the space, but apparently it is enough that our young maiden has survived the night. She must have gotten something out of the bargain, for it was she who tacitly received the unearthly visitors every Christmas Eve thereafter.

In "The Sisters and the Elves," the daughter of a devoutly syncretist household actually welcomes the merrymakers with the greeting mentioned in chapter 2: "Let them come who wish to come, and let them go who wish to go, and do no harm to me or mine." This girl, too, keeps herself to herself and keeps her nose in her Bible while the party is going on, but because she praises God when the sun comes up, the elves are forced to drop their precious gifts before they vanish. (It's all right, though: they get their treasures back again the following year when the less disciplined sister is left behind.)

The dark-minded reader will detect in the preceding stories the distant echo of human sacrifice, a seasonal gift made to the powerful elves, fairies, or land-spirits while the rest of the household looks away, and I will not say such a reader is wrong. But the more important element to recognize is the code of conduct outlined in the stories. Certainly these tales were told for entertainment—and how much more chilling they would have been when told in the darkening baðstofa or by the trembling light of an oil-fed flame at the kitchen table—but they were also teaching tools. There is another, rather daunting class of beings out there, the message runs, whose world often collides with our own. There is a good chance that someday you will encounter them, either in the borderlands or at one of those shaky times of year like Christmas and New Year's Eve, and when you do, you had better know how to handle them.

In our time, the most effective tool for banishing the otherworldly is the light switch. One flick and "Poof!"—nothing there. Like our ancestors, we perceive what we expect to perceive in the night kitchen. It's up to us to decide whether we heard the cat upsetting the dish rack or a cry for attention from the other side. For most of us, that "nothing there" is perfectly acceptable, even desirable. But there are others of us who have always hoped to perceive something more, despite the danger. The holiest night of the year is also one of the best times to send the rest of the family to church, drink a strong cup of coffee, cut the power, and wait with eyes open on the darkness.

Sitting Out 101

If your family happens to have other plans for you on Christmas Eve, there's still New Year's Eve for hobnobbing with the elves. In Sweden, December 31 was celebrated by shooting at the sky and setting off the inauspiciously named "tomte-flares," a kind of firecracker called after the little gnomelike creature that inhabits the Swedish stable. This was supposed to frighten off those ghosts, witches, and trolls who had not already departed on Christmas morning, but I'm sure the racket caused many a tomten to stick his head in the straw as well.

In sparsely populated Iceland, however, the humans were more careful. There, with the ocean on one hand and the jagged volcanic wastes of the interior on the other, the early settlers quickly realized the importance of not offending the elemental spirits who were their neighbors. Most of the time, they tried to keep well out of their way, but on December 31, a few hardy souls went looking for the Hidden Folk. In Iceland, New Year's Eve is Moving Day for the elves, so that was the best time to catch them and ask them what the future might hold.

The practice of "Sitting Out," as it was called, did not originate in Iceland but in Norway, where the ritual was enacted atop an elf-mound or deep in the forest. In the old country, it was eventually classified as witchcraft and outlawed, but the sometimes cantankerous folk who emigrated from Norway to Iceland and the Faeroe Islands tended to be the kind of people who didn't like the king telling them whether or not they could talk to the elves. Sitting Out used to take place on Christmas Eve or Twelfth Night but was transferred to New Year's Eve when January 1 became the official beginning of the year.

How to commune with the elves on New Year's Eve? It's not really all that difficult. First, you need a gray cat. Place it in a harness or cat carrier—whichever is more comfortable—because you will be taking it outside. Your kit should also include an axe, a sheepskin with gray fleece intact, and a walrus hide. If you can't get a walrus hide, the hide of an elderly ox, preferably freshly flayed, will also do. No fasting is required. I recommend a strong cup of coffee before you set off because you are going to have to stay awake all night.

Next, you must find a crossroads, all four branches of which lead directly to churches. Lay the sheepskin on the ground and yourself upon it. Cover yourself with the hide so that no part of you is visible. (Norwegian wizards skipped the sheepskin and sat on the hide, around which they inscribed nine squares in the earth, but the Icelandic instructions make no mention of this.) You must now lie perfectly still with the axe in your hands and gaze steadily at the edge of the blade, though how you're supposed to make it out in the darkness under the hide I'm not sure. In any case, you must be all in place by midnight—you'll know when it is midnight by the ringing of the church bells. Do not fall asleep; if you do, you might twitch, and you must not move any part of your body except your lips until dawn. Still staring at the edge of the axe, you can now start reciting all the incantations you learned in preparation for this occasion. Did I forget to mention that this kind of Sitting Out is only for experienced wizards?

Not to worry; there is a layman's version. When the elves encounter someone lying or sitting at a crossroads, they are compelled to stop. Anxious to get on with their move, they will first try to entice the sitter to come along with them, even assuming the shapes of his mother, sisters, or daughters. Failing that, they will offer him all sorts of wonderful gifts, and they always know just what the sitter will find most tempting. In earlier times, many a hungry Icelander was able to stare straight ahead when offered silver chalices and gold book mounts, but could not help gazing longingly at a spoonful of hot meat drippings. If you can hold out without speaking or glancing from side to side, then you can praise God aloud at first light and the elves will be forced to leave the proffered gifts behind, but no one has ever accomplished this. In fact, the sitter is often the worse for the encounter: that's how it goes when you expect to get something for nothing.

If you're not looking for treasure, and you don't particularly want to know what the future holds, you can still celebrate New Year's Eve with the elves. There were no household sprites on the Icelandic sheep farm—the little fellows never made it that far—but in the Middle Ages, a few devoted women set out food offerings at a distance from the house on New Year's Eve. They also placed extra lights about the grounds to invite the weary elves to come inside and rest their feet before traveling on to their new homestead. Back in Norway, Sitting Out took place as needed, not necessarily during the long nights of Yule, but the Icelanders' concept of an elves' moving day is specific to the Christmas season.

Though they're usually a little bit behind the times, our otherworldly brethren are not incapable of change. Moving elves might now appear as a normal-looking family with a U-Haul in tow. I would not advise inviting any unknown singletons inside your home on Christmas, New Year's, or any other eve, but if a bedraggled, slightly retro-looking clan including women and children shows up and asks for help changing a tire, don't shut the door in their faces. Once you have done them a service, you can accept any gift they offer. Whatever it is, don't throw it away; it may turn into something more valuable in the morning.

Oh, and if you're still wondering what the gray cat was for, you're going to have to summon the ghost of Icelandic folklorist Jon Arnason, who collected these instructions in the nineteenth century but never followed up on the cat.

 Craft: Elf Wreath

Some of your elvish guests may depart as soon as you've cleared your Álfablót table. Others might decide to stay for the whole festive season. Put this wreath up early and dedicate it to the elves alone. For a base, you can use grapevines or a bare ring of plastic or wood. Wrap the ring all around with a string of clear or colored lights, then wind a long strip of gauze, cheesecloth, or veiling loosely over the lights to create a softer glow. You can remove the cloth on Christmas Eve at the height of the festivities. Taking the wreath down at Twelfth Night (January 6) will be a hint to any lingering otherworldly guests that it's time to be moving along. Bid them a fond farewell and invite them to come back next year.

CHAPTER FOUR

Riders on White Horses

By early November, winter is already spreading its dark cloak over the landscape. What better time to send the children parading through the streets with pretty lights? In Germany's Protestant north, this can happen anytime during the autumn. In the Catholic south, lantern processions are centered around the larger observance of St. Martin's Day on November 11. There, the Christmas season is ushered in by the figure of St. Martin himself, riding into town on a white horse, his costume put together by the aldermen's wives in approximation of a Roman soldier, complete with helmet, horsehair crest, and scarlet cape. According to his legend, St. Martin surrendered half his cloak to a shivering beggar who turned out to be Jesus himself.

In the German saying "St. Martin comes riding on a white horse," the horse is the embodiment of the first snowfall. While the figure of the saint disappeared from pageants in the north, the horse did not. The *Schimmel*, or "white horse," consisted of one to four men under a white sheet, holding a hollow, carved head on a pole. A pot of live coals might be placed inside the head, making the mouth and eyes glow red. When the Schimmel had a rider, the whole thing was called a *Schimmelreiter* and thus became a kind of hobby horse.

Sun, Moon, and Stars

Protestant or Catholic, Martinmas lanterns are supposed to represent the light of the Christian faith, but the tiny flames are also late expressions of the bonfires that once marked winter-nights, the ancient pagan New Year at the end of October. In the old days, if you wanted to send a small child out after dark to sing and beg for sweets, you had to provide him or her with a reliable, not readily flammable or breakable, light source. Such a lantern could be made from a turnip or a *Kürbis*, a smaller, ruddier version of the American pumpkin. The lanterns were carved with frightening faces, for who knew what other creatures might be about in the frosty autumn night? Better for the children to carry their own goblins' faces, so that when the light shone out of them it would send the real goblins scuttling back into the hedgerows. And just to be on the safe side, the children themselves might dress as ghosts or other unearthly spirits.

Among farm children, both Protestant and Catholic, these customs survived into the twentieth century, while in the cities, children starting carrying Chinese paper lanterns. Today, you can buy a paper lantern ready-made for the occasion, the face decorated with the sun, moon, or stars celebrated in the old, slightly mournful folk songs that accompany the processions. Schoolchildren often make their own paper lanterns out of papier-mâché or black paper and cellophane. When the odd flare-up occurs, the lantern is simply dropped and stamped out on the cobbles.

Craft: Martinmas Lantern

The following craft features *Scherenschnitte*, a German folk art in which figures, plants, animals, and fairy-tale scenes are cut from a single sheet of paper. Scherenschnitte artists work in both black and white paper—Hans Christian Andersen was famous for his spontaneous cuttings in white—but for this project, black provides the most dramatic effect. If you use the template in this book, you should first double it in size.

Tools and materials:

- 1 sheet black paper, 9" x 12" or larger (Poster board is too thick, but construction paper will do.)
- Tracing paper
- Bristol board or thin cardboard
- Clear tape
- Glue
- Scissors
- X-Acto or other craft knife
- Hole punch
- Tea light
- 2 shish kebab skewers
- Loop of thin wire
- Long stick or dowel for carrying lantern

Martinmas lantern, figure 1

Lay the template sketch on the black paper; tape securely in place at the edges; and cut out all the white spaces with your knife. Take your time, but if you do slip up, you can make repairs with tape or glue when you mount the piece on the tracing paper.

When your picture is all cut out, coat the back with glue and mount it on the tracing paper. Smooth the piece gently with your hands to make sure all the fine details are stuck firmly to the tracing paper.

When the glue is dry, bend your work of art into a cylinder—tracing paper on the inside—and carefully close the seam with a strip of clear, strong tape. It will look best if the tape is on the inside of the cylinder.

To make the right-size base, trace the bottom of the cylinder on a piece of Bristol board. Cut out the circle, leaving a ½-inch margin all around. Cut slits all around to make tabs. Fold the tabs up, dab each tab with glue, and slide the base into the bottom of the lantern cylinder.

Glue or tape a tea light into the lantern base. When the first candle has burnt out, you can drop a new one into the same holder. But before you strike the match, punch four equidistant holes in the upper border of your lantern. These are for the shish kebab skewers to pass through.

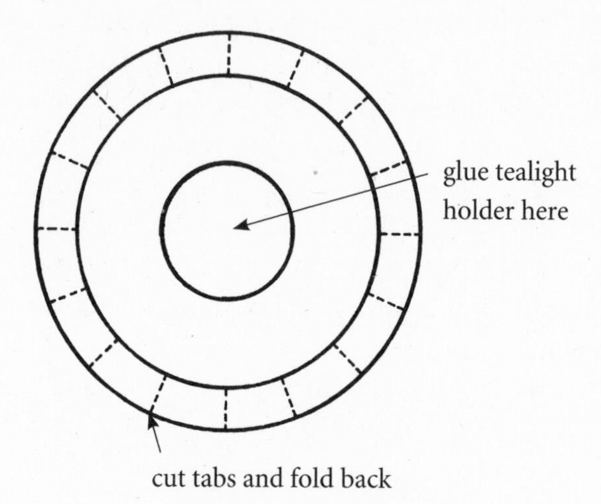

Martinmas lantern, figure 2

Now light the candle. If your lantern is tall, you will probably want to use a fireplace match. Slide the skewers through the holes and through the wire loop, being careful not to burn yourself as the heat rises up from the candle flame. Hook your carrying stick through the loop, and you're ready to set off into the dark streets.

Martinmas lantern, figure 3

Martinmas Treats

Although there is no mention of wolves in the legend of St. Martin, the Martinmas snows once brought out wolves in the form of the *Pelzmarten*, men dressed up in shaggy furs. Rather than eat the children, they threw apples to the good ones and beat the bad ones with a whip or rod. The tradition dates back to the fifteenth century at least and may be even older than the "Furry Nicks" we'll meet on St. Nicholas' Eve.

There is no mention of horns in St. Martin's legend either, but they, too, have become a part of his day. Pastries known as *Martinshoernchen*, or "little Martinmas horns," may represent the hunting horn that once belonged to the god Woden. Then again, the crescent shape might represent the moon, which can be seen bobbing in the alleys along with the sun and stars at this time of year. In bygone days, St. Martin himself was believed to enter the house on the eve of his feast day. Once inside, he turned the jug of water left out for him into wine, depositing a little horn-shaped pastry beside it when he left.

Recipe: Martinmas Horns

There is no one definitive recipe for Martinshoernchen. Some call for a yeast dough; others, like this one, call for a short pastry dough. To this day, Martinshoernchen, which are not overly sweet, are eaten as breakfast buns in the fall.

Ingredients for the dough:

- 2 sticks (one cup) unsalted butter, softened
- ¾ cup sour cream

1 egg yolk
2 Tablespoons sugar
2½ cups flour

For the filling:
1 small jar (8 oz.) apricot jam
About 3½ oz. marzipan—i.e., half a box Odense or other brand "almond candy dough"
Pinch cinnamon

For the glaze:
1 egg white

In a large bowl, mix all of the dough ingredients, adding the flour a little at a time. When the flour has all been worked in, form the dough into a ball. It will be sticky. Wrap the ball lightly in plastic wrap and refrigerate several hours or overnight.

Cut the chilled dough into four quarters. Work with one quarter at a time, leaving the rest wrapped up in the refrigerator. Roll out the dough on wax paper until it's about ⅛ inch thick or as thin as you can get it. Cut into circles with a cup or large glass.

Place the circles on a greased cookie sheet or one lined with baking parchment. Spread each one sparingly with apricot jam and sprinkle with a little cinnamon. Place a pinch of marzipan at the edge of the circle of dough, then roll the circle up with the marzipan inside. Bend the roll into a crescent or "horn," pinching the tips.

Brush horns with egg white and bake at 350°F for 20–25 minutes or until lightly browned.

The Wild Rider

The image of St. Martin as a Roman soldier never really took hold in the Anglo-Saxon realm, where another older rider on a white horse appeared in the woods at this time of year. He was known as the Wild Rider, Wild Huntsman, Hakelbarend, or simply Grim. His mount, like the cloudy November sky, was *aeppelfealo*, or "apple gray"—what later speakers of English would call "dappled." He wore a swirling cloak of blue or black homespun felted against the elements, much rougher stuff than that worn by the German Martin. Of course, none dared to touch the cloak's greasy edge as the Rider thundered past; if they knew what was good for them, they ran for cover. Those who were foolish enough to look him in the face saw that he kept half his own face covered by a floppy-brimmed hat or hood, hiding the eye that was not an eye at all but a dark, empty socket.

Before the sixth century, this ghostly huntsman would have been openly acknowledged as Woden, god of magic and the dead, retriever of the runes, of poetry and the mead that inspires it. Even after he had lost his divine status, he was treated with deference. Those living in and around the forest would have known which tracks he preferred and scrupulously avoided them when he was abroad. The lonely yeoman surprised in the woods by the croaking of ravens and the pounding of hooves knew to hide behind a shelter of nine boards or, if that were not possible, to throw himself face down on the ground and wait until the spectral hunting party had passed. Most importantly, he must not answer their hunting cry or try to engage them in conversation lest he become one of their number.

From November on through the Twelve Nights of Christmas,[13] it was wise to stay out of barns that had opposite doors, for these were the ones through which the Wild Hunt was most likely to pass. This makes perfect sense when we take into account the fact that Woden's hunting party was comprised not of the recently dead but of the long, predominantly heathen dead. A long hall with a door at each end was the construction with which these spirits were most familiar, for this was the blueprint the Angles and Saxons had brought with them from the lowlands of northern Germany. Back in the old country, the Wild Hunt left gifts behind when it passed through such houses.

Quite often, the Wild Hunt was not seen, only heard, leading some to speculate that the phenomenon was nothing more than a flock of migratory birds crying out of a cloud as they passed overhead. Even when it was "seen," the witnesses might have been observing only what the stories had led them to expect. In other words, just because it wasn't there didn't mean you couldn't see it, or be grievously harmed by it. If you failed to take the proper precautions you might be struck blind, mad, or even dead upon the passing of the Wild Rider and his ghostly retinue. At the very least, you could expect to spend several weeks in bed, recovering from the trauma.

13. This was the season in which the Wild Hunt was most commonly perceived, but the *Anglo-Saxon Chronicle* reports that in 1127, reliable witnesses (read "monks") in the area of Stamford both heard and saw the phantom hunting party go by with their black hounds and horses after February 6. The change in color is probably the result of Woden's transformation from deity to demon.

But there was also the possibility that you would be swept up, carried over the treetops, and deposited in a strange land. In the mid-nineteenth century, a Norwegian farm boy claimed to have been briefly taken up by the *Oskorei*,[14] as the Wild Hunt was sometimes known in Norway. None the worse for it, he lived to a great age, but all he could ever say of his adventure was that he had been taken to a place of splendor. Interestingly, the famous, feral Green Children of medieval East Anglia claimed to hail from "St. Martin's Land," where it was always twilight, the grass was always green, and the natives apparently ate only beans. According to a twelfth-century chronicler of wonders, the green-skinned children, a boy and a girl, had strayed into the village of St. Mary's of the Wolf-Pittes, now Woolpit, by accident, through a fissure in the earth. Was St. Martin's Land the same realm to which the Norwegian boy had been transported? Unfortunately, there is no one now living who can tell us.

"Blacker Than Pitch"

Another rider on a white horse, St. Nicholas, was of a kindlier bent. Sinterklaas, as he is known to the Dutch, starts rambling around the countryside in mid-November, well in advance of his feast day of December 6. Like Woden, Sinterklaas is old and bearded, but instead of the floppy hat, he wears a bishop's mitre. More importantly, he never goes

14. *Oskorei* comes from an Old Norse word meaning "terror," but the Norwegians had plenty of other names for this phenomenon, including *Asgardsrei*, indicating that it issued from Asgard, the abode of the Norse sky gods, and *Jolorei*, or "Yule Host." When the witch Lussi rode at its head, it was called the *Lussiferd*.

anywhere without his sidekick, Zwarte Piet or "Black Peter," whose job it is to stuff naughty children in his sack and carry them off to Spain. (In the staunchly Protestant Netherlands of the sixteenth century, a trip to sunny Catholic Spain was akin to a sojourn in Purgatory.)

In the Netherlands, Black Peter is St. Nicholas's sole attendant. Dressed in brightly colored cap or turban, his puffed sleeves peeking out from the fashionable slashings in his velvet jacket, Black Peter resembles a Moorish page boy of sixteenth-century Spain. Today, few children are afraid of this colorfully anachronistic figure. Rather than terror, he provides the comic relief to the bishop's solemn visit. Still, there can be no doubt that Black Peter has sprung from the same ageless bloodline as brasher devils like Čert and Krampus (whom we'll meet in the next chapter) and perhaps even Snorri Sturluson's pitch-black elves.

While he resembles the medieval stereotype of "the Moor," Piet's Spanish/Moorish identity has been laid over one of those dark winter spirits who were already known to emerge from the forest in the wake of the Wild Rider. And Dutch children might tell you that there is another more obvious explanation for the page's dark face: it is Black Peter's job to go up and down the sooty chimneys to fill the children's shoes so that St. Nicholas won't soil his costly bishop's robes.

Recipe: Bishop's Wine

Bisschopswijn, or bishop's wine, is drunk by the grown-ups on the feast day of St. Nicholas, Bishop of Myra, but it could just as easily have been named for St. Martin, Bishop of Tours, on whose day new wine was drunk with the Martinmas goose. Bishop's wine is just one variation of the mulled, spiced wine that is ladled out under the twinkling lights of northern Europe's outdoor Christmas markets.

Ingredients:

- 1 bottle cheap, dry red wine
- ⅓ cup vanilla sugar (This is white sugar in which a vanilla bean or two have resided for at least a few days.)
- 1 slice fresh ginger or chunk of candied ginger
- 1 star anise
- 1 cinnamon stick
- 6 cardamom pods
- 6 allspice berries
- 10 cloves
- 1 orange, sliced

Pour the wine and vanilla sugar into a large pot. Tie up the spices in a piece of cheesecloth and add to pot. Heat to simmering, stirring occasionally with a wooden spoon. Keep simmering but not boiling for about half an hour. Remove spices and float orange slices on top just before serving.

CHAPTER FIVE

Creatures of Forest and Mountain

Beware: Black Peter is not the only dark spirit abroad on the eve of St. Nicholas. Not long after the Pelzmarten has rolled up his wolf skin and hidden it at the back of the wardrobe, we hear another collection of feet tramping down the frozen track that leads out of the forest and into the village. This time, the footsteps are accompanied by the clanking of bells and the rattling of chains as well as the whistle and crack of the birch rod as it slashes through the air. There are monsters out there, and they are just warming up for their first performance.

Čert

American children know that if they start acting up early in December, they may or may not get a really good present on the morning of the twenty-fifth. The closer they get to the big day, the less the threat of an empty or briquette-filled stocking becomes, because hasn't Santa already packed up his sleigh? What a nuisance it would be for him to have to dig down through all those packages to retrieve one light-up fighting hamster–bot just because someone forgot to clean her room. Yes, the sad truth is that there is very little left of real fear in the twenty-first-century American Christmas.

But fear is alive and well among Czech children on the eve of St. Nicholas Day, known to them as Angels and Devils Night. The star of Angels and Devils Night is a horned demon named Čert who looks rather like an upright goat but has the face and hands of a man, and whose foot-long scarlet tongue will prevent you from ever mistaking him for Mr. Tumnus. His wrists linked by iron chains, he carries a birch switch in one hand and an empty basket on his back. Thanks to Čert, Czech children do not have to wait until Christmas Eve to get what's coming to them; as the sun sets on December 5, they face the very real possibility that they will be carried off to Hell in Čert's basket that very night.

If Čert, or Krampus as he is known in Austria and parts of Germany, were allowed to roam freely, we would all be lost. Fortunately, he always appears in the company of a starched white angel and St. Nicholas himself in full Myran bishop's regalia. Usually, if not always, the angel intercedes on the child's behalf. St. Nicholas hands out a few small gifts, and the party departs the home with Čert rattling his chains and grumbling over his bad luck. Still, he has this to comfort him: though not the last goat-man we'll meet in these pages, he is certainly the most frightful, and the one who has managed to hold on to his devilish form the longest.

Knecht Ruprecht

Another of Čert's German cousins, Knecht[15] Ruprecht, dresses like a Trappist monk. Though he shrinks from the spotlight, Knecht Ruprecht reached the pinnacle of fame in 1862 by way of a poem by north German poet/novelist Theodor Storm. Since then, "Knecht Ruprecht" has been recited before many a German Tannenbaum on Christmas Eve. Recite the opening line, "Von drauss' vom Wald komm ich her. . . " ("From out of the forest I now appear . . ."[16]), to any north German native, and he or she will be unable to resist rattling off the rest of the poem. Rather than a devil who must be restrained, Storm's Knecht Ruprecht is the dedicated helper of the Christ Child. In fact, it is the Christ Child who checks that his right-hand man has both his sack and his rod before they set off on their business.

Knecht Ruprecht is now more usually to be found in the company of St. Nicholas. He wears a black or brown robe with a pointed hood and in Catholic regions might carry a rosary. He is always bearded and often soot-smudged as well, though these are clearly the ashes of the penitent that streak his face. All in all, his foreboding presence is like that of Dickens's Ghost of Christmas Yet to Come, but instead of pointing a bony finger, Knecht Ruprecht carries a bundle of birch twigs.

15. *Knecht* is a false cognate for the English "knight"; it means "farmhand" or "servant."
16. Denis Jackson's complete English translation of "Knecht Ruprecht" can be found at www.theodorstorm.co.uk.

Don't let the monk's robes fool you; Knecht Ruprecht's name, from Old High German *Hruodperaht*, suggests that he was once the servant of the goddess "Perahta," or Perchta.

Other Nicholases

One would imagine that St. Nicholas and his villainous sidekicks must occupy opposite ends of the spectrum, but this has not always been the case. The frightful and the benevolent came together, or had yet to part ways, in the furry person of the Pelznichol, who could be distinguished from his brother Pelzmartl only by name and timing of appearance. Close cousins to both were Ruklaus (Rough Claus) and Aschenklaus (Ashy Claus). All had been christened with variations of the saint's name, but there was nothing saintly about them. They all liked to beat children with birch rods, except for Aschenklaus; in his hand the saint's crosier had devolved into a walking stick to the top of which he had knotted a bag full of ashes. It was with this that he clobbered naughty children, turning them just as ashy as himself.

These "Nicholases" all brought gifts as well as instruments of corporal punishment, but they never pressed the nuts and apples into the eager children's hands; they strewed them over the ground or floor as the medieval Pelzmarten had done before them. This strewing may be one of the most ancient rituals of the season. In eastern Lithuania, the father of the house used to scatter different kinds of grain over the farmhouse floor on the Eve of Epiphany. The children gathered the grains in their laps, then sorted them to see which crop would fare best that year.

The Dream of the Rod

In the old days, most children experienced more than just the threat of a beating on St. Nicholas' Eve. Before they could pick up their treats, it was compulsory to feel the sting of those birch twigs across the backs of their fingers. The apples and nuts that the Pelznichol brought have long been recognized as tokens of fertility, and so has the kiss of the lash. The birch rod, as wielded at Christmastime, functioned more as a magic wand than as an instrument of pain. From England to Austria, the apple trees themselves were beaten in winter, and *they* certainly hadn't done anything wrong. Rather than being "beaten into submission," the recipient of the blow was beaten into long life, good health, and productivity. In Finland to this day, Christmas Eve would not be complete without a good switching with a handful of leafy birch twigs in the sauna.

Sometimes, the Pelznichol would simply scatter the rods along with the goodies, while the stealthier St. Nicholas will tie a few twigs to the gifts as a matter of course so that the child waking in the morning will know that *he knows.* In early Protestant Germany, the treats were tucked inside the bundle of rods left by the Christ Child. All of these token twigs may have survived from the very Christmaslike Roman festival of Kalends, when pagan Romans exchanged *strenae* to mark the beginning of the New Year in January. In later times, these strenae took the form of sweetmeats, little clay lamps, and coins bearing the double visage of the god Janus, but originally strenae were branches cut from a sacred laurel grove belonging to Strenia, goddess of vigor. The message conveyed by both the sticks and the more substantial gifts was the same: the giver wished the recipient to enjoy a year of light, warmth, wealth, good health, and good things to eat.

Of course, none of this prevented nightmares of the dreaded rod from interfering with the sugar plums dancing in children's heads as St. Nicholas Day approached. The Pelznichol eventually faded away, so in those regions that did not enjoy the services of a Krampus or Knecht Ruprecht, the saint himself was left holding the *Rute*,[17] as it is called in German. It is only right that this magic wand should have passed at last into the hands of St. Nicholas, whose full title is St. Nicholas Thaumaturgus, a worker of wonders.

European postcards of the Victorian era make it clear that the switch was nothing less than a ritual tool. While sometimes it is a simple bunch of birch twigs stripped of their leaves and bound once or twice with osiers at the base, it is just as often gilded or festooned with colorful little flags. It might be the size of a bottle brush or as bushy as a small tree. This year, as the fifth of December approaches, allow yourself to be inspired by the shopkeepers of central Europe who decorate their windows with birch twigs dressed up in tinsel and tiny white light bulbs. Done right, an oversized *Rute* can take the place of a tabletop Christmas tree. And nothing says "I know what you've been up to, but I love you anyway" like a bundle of twigs tipped with gold glitter and studded with chocolates.

17. *Rute* comes from the same root as *rood*, the Old English term for the cross on which Christ died.

The Buttnmandl

We turn now from the shop windows of the town to follow the jangle of cowbells up into the shadow of the Berchtesgadener Alps, where the very Sendakian rumpus starts on December 5. Even now, bobbing human bundles of straw known as *Buttnmandln* are descending through the twilight of St. Nicholas' Eve to "surprise" their fellow villagers. Each Buttnmandl is strapped round the waist with three deafening cowbells—two small, one large—which can be heard more than a mile away, so there's really no surprise at all. They are preceded by the good saint, a white-robed angel or Christ Child figure, and several devils dressed in furs and Krampus masks. Though the straw effectively obscures their faces, the Buttnmandln, too, wear masks. These ritual masks are known as *Larven* in German, instead of the more usual *Masken*. *Larve* comes from Latin *larva*, which denotes both a mask and an unquiet ghost.[18]

Stopping at the first house in the village, St. Nicholas delivers his sermon and his gifts. Both the devils and the straw monsters try to wait patiently until the old man has finished, but a few of them can't help twirling their long whips of braided leather. As soon as the saint has finished, they step in, grab whichever unmarried girls happen to be hanging about, carry them outside, and tumble them in the snow. Hint to the girls: though massive, the Buttnmandl is

18. The carving of these *Larven* is a folk art, but some of the inspiration may have come from the fanciful and sometimes frightful Romanesque carvings in which Berchtesgaden abounds. The St. Peter and St. Johannes Cloister contains a part-human, part-leonine stone visage whose generous tongue, like that of the Krampus, extends well beyond his teeth.

easily overpowered—knock him over and he can't get up again. The fur-clad devils, however, are harder to outrun.

Devils with outthrust tongues, young bachelors dressed as harvested stands of grain, brandishing long whips as they pursue their girlfriends: it's hard to miss the fertility aspects of the *Buttnmandllauf*, which translates roughly as "Running of the Riddle-Raddle Men." Happily, these living wheat sheaves are still running strong today. If you happen to be in the Berchtesgadener Alps on the evening of December 5 and hear the discordant ringing of cowbells, you'll know you'll soon be greeted by the sight of this rustling parade. Though both devils and Buttnmandln are blessed with holy water before they set out, they belong to a religion much older than Christianity. I think old Berchta, whose Alps these are, must be pleased at how well the monsters have held up.

The Bells of St. Nicholas

With the exception of Black Peter in his newfangled page's costume, none of these frightful characters would think of leaving the house without their bells on. The wearing of bells and other jangling things is a universal means of protecting the wearer from evil or simply opportunistic spirits. There are those who would regard the copper bells sewn on a Siberian shaman's tunic as the precursors of the harness bells worn by Santa's reindeer, with the Pelznichol bridging the chronological gap. If you are going to follow that line of thinking, then you should probably also count Moses's brother Aaron, whose priestly skirts were trimmed with little golden bells, among Santa's direct ancestors.

The truth is that with very little effort, a bell can be made to tinkle prettily or jangle incessantly: it makes music practically all by itself. This must have seemed nothing short of magic to the ancients, especially when we consider that bells are made of metal, a material that was itself brought into being through an apparently magical process. Wherever there have been bells, they have been used to ward off unseen and undesirable influences.

Because they wear bells, and because they spare not the rod with all its inherent blessings, we must accept the fact that these rough and often hideous creatures that come bounding out of the forest at the onset of winter are not at all evil. We have already witnessed the demotion of the god Woden to ghostly huntsman and watched the elves grow small. Could the attendants of St. Nicholas be cast-down fertility gods? Or do they descend from the *Svartálfar*, those dark elves about which Snorri Sturluson had so little to say? While they may never have ranked as high as the light elves, these dark spirits were apparently indispensable. Rather than force a tenuously Christianized community to do without them, the Church sprinkled them with holy water and incorporated them into the saint's retinue, where they remain to this day.

St. Nicholas's triumphant entry into Amsterdam each year would seem strange without Black Peter loping along beside the bishop's white horse. Children in Central Europe still hide under the furniture when Čert or Krampus comes tramping in, and German children hide behind their parents at the first glimpse of Knecht Ruprecht. As for the Pelznichol, he did not go quietly but got his rambunctious second wind in the New World.

The Bellsnickle

The Pelznichols were among the first dark Christmas spirits to make it to North America. As soon as they got off the boat, many of them doffed their fur coats and put on patched jackets instead. As the new spellings of their name attest, the most important part of the Bellsnickle's, Bellschniggle's, or Bellsneakle's costume was now the harness of sleigh bells. Back in the Rhineland, they had already disentangled themselves from the date of December 6, which is, after all, a saint's feast day and therefore not in the spirit of Protestantism. Those who were engaged to make house calls now did so on Christmas Eve.

Also present in Nova Scotia and West Virginia, the Bellsnickle was the dominant strain in the eighteenth-to-early-nineteenth-century Pennsylvania Christmas. When the German Bellsnickles met up with the Celtic ritual of mumming, the two traditions merged, but the new one retained the name of "belsnickling." Along with the Bellsnickle came the Christ-Kindel, whose name is a dialectical shortening of *Christkindlein*, the Baby Jesus, but who was usually imagined looking more like an angel. While in some parts of Pennsylvania the Christ-Kindel remained the silent, stealthy gift-giver whom good children expected to fill their baskets by Christmas morning, he eventually developed an alter-ego, the Kris Kinkle.[19] Although the Kris Kinkle never gave up his

19. Further dialectical developments would produce "Kris Kringle," which had become a synonym for Santa Claus by 1845.

name, he soon shed his white nightshirt for the Bellsnickle's get-up: a makeshift mask or face blackened with burnt cork, a tow wig, and plenty of bells either sewn or strapped on.

Adjectives used to describe these Bellsnickles and Kris Kinkles in the newspapers and diaries of the day include "hideous," "horrid," "frightful," and "abominable." Imagine such a face appearing at your window as darkness fell on Christmas Eve. The typical Bellsnickle announced his arrival by tapping at the glass pane with his fat birch switch or slender rod. Many of them also carried whips. The Bellsnickle always knew who had been naughty. When he entered the house, he scattered hard cookies and candies like chicken feed over the floor where the good children were allowed to gather them up. The other children had to dodge the switch or whip in order to snatch their prizes. At first, the Bellsnickle received no payment during his visit; the parents settled up with him behind the scenes. Under the influence of the mummers, however, the Bellsnickle, who was usually a teenage boy, began to expect wine, cider, cakes, and even money when he showed up at the door.

Each neighborhood really only needed one Bellsnickle, but that did not stop other young men disguising themselves and roving the snowy countryside just for fun. Soon, the streets were filling up with young ruffians whom the townsfolk had begun to find annoying rather than enchanting. Once belsnickling lost its parental stamp of approval, it devolved into a Halloweenish gathering of local youths who rambled through the streets in off-the-rack costumes.

The Yule Lads

Iceland, too, has its share of frightful creatures roaming the farms at Advent, but they don't start showing their faces until six days after St. Nicholas Day, which is a non-event in much of Scandinavia. They are the *Jólasveinar*, the "Yule Swains" or "Christmas Lads," who begin their official invasion of Iceland on December 12. Thirteen days before Christmas, the first of these Yule Lads descends from the mountains, a new one appearing each day to hang about the farmstead or even the streets of Reykjavik until there are thirteen of them making merry on Christmas Day.

If you look out the window after dark and see a trollish lad making faces back at you, that would be Window Peeper. Have the smoked mutton and *skyr* that you put aside for Christmas dinner disappeared? Blame Meat Hooker and Skyr Gobbler. Someone clattering among the dirty dishes in the sink? The culprits would be Pot Scraper, Spoon Licker, and Bowl Licker. You don't have to guess what kind of mischief Skirt Blower likes to get up to, but some of the lads have more enigmatic names such as Door Sniffer, Candle Beggar, and Gully Gawk. While folklorist Jon Arnason standardized their number in 1864—before that there could be as many as twenty and as few as nine—their names still vary.

In the Icelandic folktale "See My Grey Foot Dangle," three children are left home alone while their parents attend church on Christmas Eve. They've each been given a candle and a pair of bright red socks, which they sit around admiring when a voice is heard out in the yard. The youngest and therefore most innocent child remarks that it must be Jesus who is calling to them through the window. The boy's use of the holy name banishes the creature, who was not Jesus at all but a hairy, gray Icelandic troll who would surely have spirited one or more of the children away. Was this troll one of the Yule Lads? He might have been, for in the old days, the Yule Lads often had children on their grocery list.

You can't really blame the lads for their bad habits. Their parents were the trolls Gryla and Leppaludi, though Gryla may actually have borne them all out of wedlock. We don't know much about Leppaludi, but Gryla was a great eater of children. The Christmas Lads have been around since at least the 1600s, and the years have been kind to them. They used to be ogres as terrible as their parents but are now merely oafish. These days, they like to dress like Santa Claus and are inclined to bring presents instead of carrying children off and dropping them in their mother's pot. In the 1920s, Icelandic children started placing their shoes in the window anytime after December 12 in the expectation that the Yule Lads would fill them.

Goblins at the Window

Although it was not written down until a month after the fact, the following incident occurred on or around November 21, 1933, according to Father Nicholas Christmas, who included it in a letter to the children of J. R. R. Tolkien in December of that year. (The letter can now be read by all in the book *Letters from Father Christmas*, edited by Baillie Tolkien.) On the night in question, Father Christmas was woken by a disturbing "squeak and spluttering" in his bedroom, followed by the appearance of a "wicked little face" at the window, which was some distance above the ground. There was no doubt about it: the old man's Cliff House was under attack from bat-riding goblins.

In the Scandinavian literature of which Tolkien was so fond, the goblins are always hungry for treasure. In the Norwegian tale "The Christmas Visitors at Kvame," the goblin chieftain, Old Trond, brings his own silver goblets to the party at a Norwegian farmhouse and is only parted from his treasures when he is shot dead in the High Seat.[20] Old Trond would have been subordinate to the Goblin King, who lived in Sweden and presided over a considerably larger hoard of golden chalices, coins, and plates. The nastier the goblin, the greater the hoard, and the Norwegian *jutul* was the nastiest of all. On Christmas Eve, if you were brave enough to venture into the mountains, you could see glow of the jutul's treasure-heap blazing out from the cracks in the rock face with the brilliance of a thousand candles.

The goblins of the North Pole, however, are mad for toys—especially the toys Father Christmas stores in the cellars of his Cliff House. In fact, they will do anything to get their clumsy black paws on the train sets and are apparently untroubled by the steel components, unlike their more traditional cousins who cannot tolerate iron in any of its forms. As Father Christmas reports to the children, the use of green smoke had failed to eradicate the goblins the year before, and now they've grown especially bold.

20. In the Scandinavian home, the ornately carved High Seat was reserved for the master of the household. By breaking in and seating himself there, Old Trond was displaying typical goblin cheek.

In none of the Scandinavian tales do the goblins have wings, nor do those besieging the Cliff House. When Father Christmas glimpses them in the darkness outside his window, he comes to the immediate conclusion that they are riding on bats. Why bats? Why not some more plausible species such as the snowy owl or a high-stepping Arctic hare? Although rare—F. C.'s staff had not seen a goblin on a bat since 1453—the bat-riding Christmas spirit is not without precedent.

When Father Christmas, with the help of his compatriots, Polar Bear and the Red Gnomes, finally got the upper hand and drop-kicked the goblins' noxious little corpses out the door, he sat down to paint a picture of the battle, which is how we know that the North Pole goblins are soot-black, the usual color of troublesome Christmas spirits as well as a few of the beneficent ones. John Grossman's album of antique postcards, *Christmas Curiosities: Odd, Dark, and Forgotten Christmas*, includes the antitheses of these polar goblins: a handful of rosy-cheeked angelic little boys riding their own bridled bats—noctules and pipistrelles, by the looks of them. Each chubby boy is wearing a jockey's outfit and holding what appears to be a peacock feather. They are coming to wish us all a "bright New Year," but the tiny white wings sprouting from their backs are the only even faintly seasonal symbol in sight. (The wings naturally raise the question of why these boys need to be riding bats at all!)

The bat would not appear seasonal to us, but this color lithograph was printed in 1895, about the same time that a three-year-old J. R. R. Tolkien first arrived in England from his birthplace in South Africa, a time when the idea that

Christmas and New Year's belonged, in part, to the squeaky creatures of the night could still sell a few postcards. (Grossman's album also features a tribe of fur-clad fairies roasting a rat over an open fire and a coven of witches scattering Christmas wishes while flying backward on their broomsticks.)

Even at Halloween, bats have never been as popular as black cats, so it's unlikely they'll ever become the official mascots of Christmas. They seem to have fallen out of favor with the goblins too, for no further incidents of aerial batmanship have been reported since that infamous night in 1933. Still, you never know, so keep an eye on your stash of Christmas presents and be alert for any flapping or squeaking at the attic window.

CHAPTER SIX

The Scandinavian Household Sprite

If you are not already in possession of a household sprite, you should think very carefully before taking one on. The English version of the household sprite is the boggart, and the most famous boggart was probably the one belonging to the Yorkshire Gilbertsons. Fed up with their boggart's mischievous pranks, the Gilbertsons decided to move house. The cart was all packed up and ready to go when they heard the boggart speak up from inside the butter churn. "We're flittin'," he explained to an inquisitive neighbor. It had never even occurred to the boggart that the family might try to leave without him.

Rather than stay behind in an empty house or, worse yet, get used to a new family, the household sprite will stick with those he knows. Conditioned by centuries of primogeniture, the *nisse*, *tomten*, or *tonttu* will usually cast his lot with the eldest son—that is, the one most likely to inherit the old homestead. There was a time when no farm in Denmark, Sweden, Norway, or Finland was without its tiny, bright-eyed old man to help with the chores at night. Over the last few hundred years, many of these creatures have moved to the cities, especially in Denmark, which has the highest concentration of household sprites. In the Faeroe Islands, the chores were sometimes taken over by the red-capped *niðagrisur* (see "The Yule Boar" in chapter 8), while in Iceland there are only the *huldrefolk*, who have no special attachment to the farmstead. Since it was not only second sons traveling to Iceland at the time of settlement,[21] this indicates that the household sprite is either reluctant to travel far from his homeland or, like the Celtic fairy, is unable to cross large bodies of water.

Still, accidents and exceptions do happen, so if you are of Scandinavian descent, there is a remote chance that you might already have one of the old fellows living in your home. The information in the following pages should help you to identify him and make him more comfortable. If your family does not hail from that part of the world, or if you come from a side branch of the family, it's not too late to acquire your own domestic goblin. The best place to do so is at a Scandinavian Christmas market. While there

21. There is an episode early in the Icelandic *Laxdaela Saga* in which the matriarch Unn the Deep-Minded recovers the High Seat pillars, which she had brought from Norway and lost when her ship was wrecked in Iceland. She decides to build her house right there where the carved pillars have washed ashore. Had her household sprite been carried along with them, she might have expected to find a fire already burning, the turves for the house walls cut, and the horses fed and combed, but this was not the case. Earlier, Unn had left her granddaughter Olof behind in the Faeroe Islands. Olof was to become the progenitoress of the mighty Gotuskeggi clan, so it is possible that the family nisse stayed with her and was later conflated with the Faroese niðagrisur.

is nothing intrinsically Christmassy about the boggart, the nisse, tomten, and tonttu are the epitome of Yule. Yes, you could order one online, but picking them up in your hands and patting their knitted caps will help you to choose the one that's right for you. Failing this, you can follow the instructions at the end of this chapter and make your own.

A homemade house-sprite is not just a consolation prize but a long-standing practice. Medieval Germans were carving little kobolds out of boxwood back in the thirteenth century, ostensibly just for fun but originally as objects of veneration. In Scandinavia, the carving of these creatures is now a specialized craft. (No doubt our ancestors would be surprised how popular the wooden trolls have become!)

Jacob Grimm assures us that household sprites can indeed be bought and sold, but if you are the third pair of hands to receive one, you must hold on to it forever. Grimm identified all of these tutelary spirits, along with the kobold, with the ancestral ghosts who dwelt in the hearth and liked to use it as a front door. There is no denying that the household sprite has come down in the world. Assuming that he is indeed of the same lineage as those age-old spirits of the fireplace, he resides there no longer. At some point, he was moved to the periphery of the home, to the attic, stable, or barn, and the daily repast that was set out for him became a once-a-year treat. Household sprites are not all cut from the same homespun; there are subtle differences in their dress, characters, and preferences. We'll begin our study with the nisse, whose kind covers the largest area: both Norway and Denmark.

Nisse

Nisse may be derived from *Nicholas* and thus a generic nickname, but the nisse has never really had anything to do with St. Nicholas Day; Christmas Eve is his special night. The farm nisse used to be particular about Thursdays: there was to be no spinning or chopping of firewood on a Thursday night, a reflection of his heathen leanings.[22]

The Norwegian farm nisse was once restricted to the southeastern part of the country. The northern and western districts were the territory of the *gardvord* and the somewhat more crotchety *tunkall*. The earliest gardvord was a giant who could hold his own against any troll. Because he was too big to fold himself up in the hayloft, he was given the use of an empty room or outbuilding. He allowed himself to be seen more often than the nisse, while the tunkall appeared to and conversed only with the elderly. Most likely, the tunkall or the gardvord was the ghost of some old grandfather, perhaps the one who had established the farm and vowed never to leave it.

A descendant of the gardvord and tunkall, the nisse is now drastically shrunken. The German kobold was supposed to be the size of a four-year-old child, but the nisse is only as tall as a one-year-old. When he chooses to doff his red cap, thereby making himself visible, you can see that he has a long gray beard. The city nisse might wear a red

22. Not every nisse is a heathen. Each church used to have its own *kirkegrim*, or church nisse. Though identical to the farm nisse and often believed to be a specialized breed of the same, the kirkegrim is more likely to be the lingering ghost of a foundation sacrifice.

or blue suit, but the farm nisse wears a smock and trousers of natural-colored wool. Though they're quite scuffed and ordinary-looking, his buckled shoes can carry him over mountains and bogs at terrific speeds. The Christmas market nisse tends to stoutness, even cuddliness, but the old-time farm nisse is simply an old man in miniature.

Though child-sized, he prefers adult company, when he wants company at all. He does not like his routine disrupted. If he catches you spying on him while he's doing his chores, he will desert you no matter how much it pains him to do so. When making his nocturnal rounds, he carries a lantern with a blue flame in it. His work finished, he retires either to the hayloft, stable, cellar, or oldest tree in the yard. The careless snapping of even one branch of this tree will also force him to leave the farm. Since he does his work under cover of darkness, he must sleep through the long days of summer. He gets up again around Michaelmas (September 29), when he switches his pointed cap for a round one, just for the day.

The Norwegian nisse avoids the sun but loves the moonlight, especially as reflected by the hard crust of the snow. Still spry, he enjoys all the usual winter sports—he may look like he's on his last legs, but his strength and agility will surprise you. Another of the nisse's idiosyncrasies is his preference for black horses. On the farm, one horse, usually a black mare, will appear particularly well cared for, her coat gleaming, her mane combed and even braided when no one is looking. If such a horse is sold, the nisse will go with her.

On Christmas Eve, it is imperative that you serve your nisse a bowl of porridge with a fat pat of butter in the middle. The Norwegian nisse also likes cake and beer. Unlike the English brownie or Robin Goodfellow, he has no problem with clothes. For a Christmas present, you can't go wrong with a new red cap with a tassel at the point or a jacket fringed with tiny bells, but don't give him anything as fine as a pair of white leather breeches; he will think them too nice to work in, and you'll have to do all the chores yourself.

At first glance, you might not be able to tell the Danish nisse from the Norwegian, for the only difference is the absence of the tassel on the Danish nisse's cap. Denmark's Jutland peninsula once had the most household sprites per square mile. Consequently, it is the Jutish nisse who now defines the breed. He is of a petulant bent, and, like his Norwegian cousin, he is not fond of children. At Christmastime he might carry a birch switch tucked in his sash. He takes excellent care of the livestock, even stealing from the neighbors to give them extra grain. His best friend is the family cat, but he also gets along with the pine martens and other creatures that winter among the rafters. Dogs bark at him, which is one of the reasons he likes to keep out of sight, though he is not above sitting on a window ledge and swinging his feet just out of reach of the dog's snapping teeth.

The Jutish nisse might inhabit any dark space on the farm. In the city, he prefers the attic or a spot near the chimney, so perhaps he is not so far removed from the old hearth spirits after all. He is devoted to the family but often at odds with the maids and farmhands. If they tease him, he will take his revenge by yanking off the blankets while they are sleeping, throwing them in the well, or blackening their faces with soot from the fireplace.

Thomas Keightley, writing in 1850, mentions the Jutish nisse's daily meal of *groute*, a sweet porridge of hulled oats or wheat grains, but I would not advise serving your nisse oatmeal on Christmas Eve. His tastes have become quite refined over the years, and he now prefers the Frenchified *ris a l'amande*, a sweet rice pudding made with almonds, whipped cream, and sherry. Because he is a humble fellow at heart, you should serve it to him in a wooden bowl with a wooden spoon. If you can only manage a basic rice porridge (recipe follows), be sure the butter pat is cold enough that he will have time to notice it before it melts and trickles to the bottom of the bowl. If he thinks there is no butter in his porridge, he will throw a tantrum.

Though easily peeved, the Jutish nisse is usually sorry for it afterward, and there are few things you could do that would make him desert the family. There is a story of a particularly prankish Jutish nisse who drove his master and family to move house. The story ends just like that of the Gilbertsons' boggart, but in this case the nisse, popping his head out of a washtub, is plainly visible.

Tomten

In the picture-book version of Viktor Rydberg's *The Christmas Tomten*, the titular hero looks in on a family absorbed in the Gospel of St. Luke and remarks to his orphan companion, "I'm very fond of that baby he is reading about . . . But mind you, old Thor was a fine fellow too." It's not surprising, then, that when Thor's goat, the *Julbok*, went into retirement in the mid-1800s, the tomten took over his gift-giving duties in Sweden. Harald Wiberg's pencil and watercolor illustrations for *The Christmas Tomten* reveal a barrel-shaped, bandy-legged old man whose white beard touches his toes and whose eyes glow like a cat's in the moonlight. Though the top of his head does not even reach the doorknob, his nose and hands belong to a much larger creature. His fingertips brush the crust of the snow when he walks, as does the tassel on the point of his stocking cap.

The visual artists of the turn of the twentieth century were in accord with Wiberg about the tomten's white beard, though he often went without the tassel in the Christmas postcards of the period. In place of the nisse's magic buckled shoes, the tomten wears gray stockings and wooden clogs, the better to make his way across the snowy yard. If he wants to get somewhere fast, he borrows the farmer's sleigh.

Many a tomten abides in the *botrae*, an ancient tree that grows before the farmhouse door. This is usually a linden, ash, or elm, but the earliest botrae may have been a crab-apple tree.[23] In another, larger life, which the tomten now only dimly remembers, he planted the tree himself. *Tomt* refers to the packed earth that lies underneath the buildings of the farmstead and extends into the square courtyard. Thus, the tomten, or *tomte-gubbe*, "old man about the grounds," is the least likely to emigrate. His bones are older even than the beams holding up the walls, and he identi-

23. For more about the botrae, or *apaldr* as it was known to the Norsemen, see my article "The Golden Apples of Jotunheim," in *Llewellyn's 2013 Herbal Almanac.*

fies himself with the very ground upon which his house is built.

Surround the tomten's Christmas porridge with a moat of honey in addition to the butter pat on top, and he will be especially pleased. The best place to leave his meal is in the stable, for he prefers the company of the livestock. The gifts presented to him on Christmas morning should include a length of gray homespun out of which he will presumably make his own clothes, a pinch of tobacco, and as much clay as a spade can hold. This last is either a token of his chthonic nature, the material for making a pipe, or an acknowledgment that it was he who laid the first shovelful of earth in the house walls.

Tonttu

Like the tomten, the Finnish tonttu is a pipe smoker. He doesn't mind a glass of brandy alongside his rice porridge either. You can put his Christmas Eve meal in the sauna, the seat of both physical and spiritual cleanliness in the Finnish home. The Finns themselves like to dress up as *Joulutonttuja*, "Yule tonttus," in red cotton caps with bells at their points, and they are most fond of dressing up little girls in the full kit: red cap, red suit, striped scarf, and stockings. That's all right for the Joulutonttuja cavorting in the shopping districts—Finland needs a spark of color at this time of year—but I would guess that the ancient little man sipping his brandy in the sauna dresses more soberly.

If you have never seen a tonttu, it is because he does not spend very much time above ground. His real home is a glittering world inside the earth. Some tonttu did not come with the farm but had to be fetched from the churchyard. Once he had been brought home, he had to be given his own room with his own bed and dinner table. That done, he would make sure the family prospered.

There seems to be a genetic link between the tonttu and the *kirkonwaki*, or "church folk," a misshapen little people who dwell in the shadow of the altar cloth. The kirkonwaki's misshapenness marks him as a *seite*, a suggestively formed stone or tree stump that served as an object of veneration among the pre-Christian Finnic peoples. The most unusual thing about the kirkonwaki is the existence of females among them. The reason there are not more kirkonwaki in the world is because these females have difficulty giving birth. When his wife goes into labor, the kirkonwaki will seek out a Christian woman to come and assist her with a laying on of hands, suggesting that the kirkonwaki are not Christians themselves. As payment, the mortal woman is rewarded with gifts of silver and gold.

Jacob Grimm relates the same story as told in Sweden. Here, the distressed husband is described only as "a little man with a black face." For her trouble, the Christian midwife receives "old silver vessels." If not for the story's pedigree—it's an example of Migratory Legend 5070—one would have to wonder if the whole thing had not been a fabrication to explain away the presence of church treasures in a house where they did not belong.

The Resilient Sprite

It would be simplistic to say that the nisse, tomten, and tonttu are the diminished spirits of the dead and nothing more. For one thing, a belief in these often comical little creatures coexisted for a time with the larger gardvord and tunkall. Their capers also overlapped with the more serious idea that both the recently and the long and nameless dead visited their old homes on Christmas Eve.

As part of a ritual once prevalent throughout Europe, the table was laid for the ghostly visitors; candles were left burning for their enjoyment; and, in some cases, the living vacated their beds to allow the ancestors a good night's sleep before the bells began to toll on Christmas morning. In Celtic lands, this ritual was enacted at Halloween, while in the Nordic, Finnic, and Baltic realms, it was eventually absorbed into Yule. In Scandinavia, it may once have been part of the late autumn Álfablót and Dísablót observances.

The folktales in which the Scandinavian household sprite appears have much in common with the stories of kobolds, boggarts, and brownies elsewhere, but the sprite himself is unique in the details of his clothing, his preferences, and his close but often frustrated relationship with the rest of the household. He is, I think, a Christian society's grudgingly affectionate remembrance of its heathen dead as viewed through a prism of humor and imagination. The gardvord, tunkall, and hungry Christmas ghost have all faded away, but the little old man about the grounds is as active as ever.

Craft: Christmas Tomten

No matter how many of these little fellows you make, you will find that each has its own personality. The grain of the wood will suggest a face; there is no need to draw one. Why plaster a smile on a creature who, like you, may not feel cheerful all the time?

Since each tomten's pointy hat is a quarter of a circle, you might as well make four of them at a clip. There is only room for one tomten in a household, so give the others away.

Tools and materials (per tomten):

One 1-inch-diameter plain wooden bead for the body
One ¾-inch-diameter plain wooden bead for the head
White acrylic paint
Color acrylic paint: red, dark blue, or soft gray
Paintbrush
Glue

Paper for hat:

Use a paper with a bit of nap, nothing smooth or shiny. Washi—high quality Japanese origami paper—in a solid color works very well. This usually comes in packs of square 5⅞-inch sheets.
Scissors
Pipe cleaner
Cotton ball

Paint the larger bead with a base coat of white. When dry, paint with color. Glue the smaller bead on for the head and set aside (figure 1).

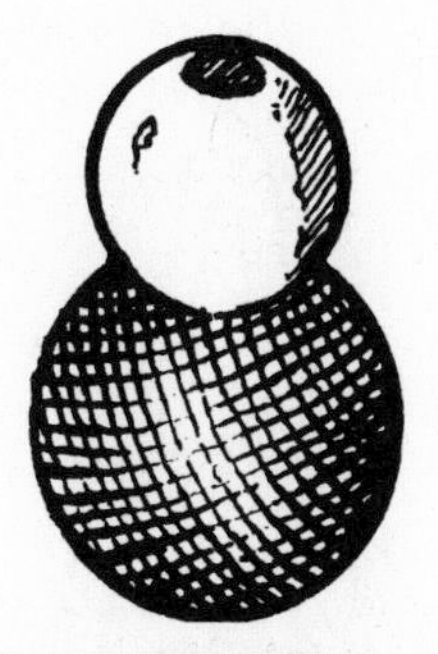

Christmas tomten, figure 1

Cut a 4⅛-inch-diameter circle out of your paper. Fold the circle into quarters and cut along the creases. One quarter equals one hat. Crumple the paper gently to give it a softer, clothlike look (figure 2). Now roll it into a tall, skinny cone and glue the seam (figure 3). Glue the base of the hat to the tomten's head.

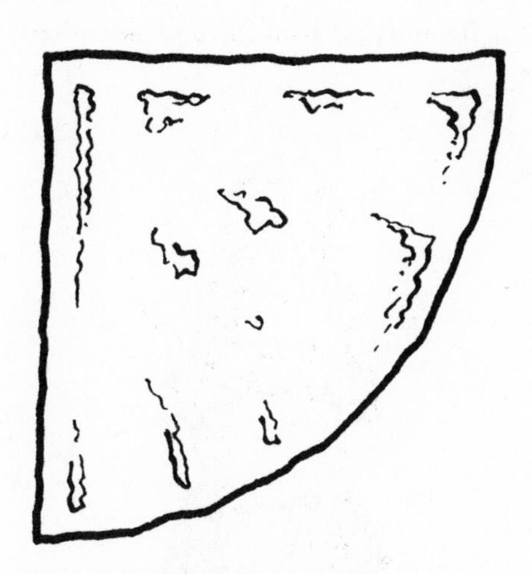

Christmas tomten, figure 2

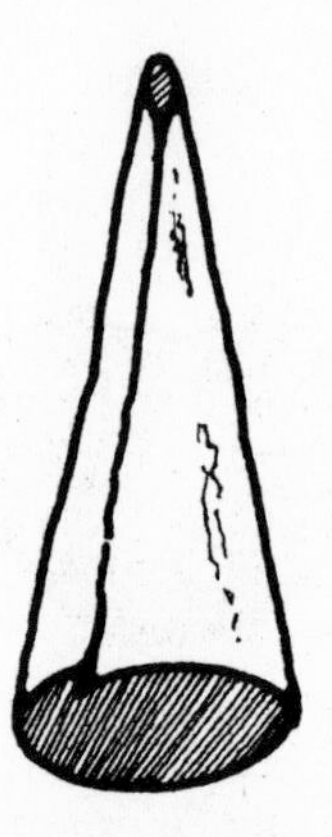

Christmas tomten, figure 3

While the glue is drying, cut a 3½-inch length of pipe cleaner and twist it into a ring. This is the fur trim on your tomten's cap. Slip it on and secure with a few dabs of glue. Fold the point of the cap over and glue down.

Pull a wisp from the cotton ball and glue on for the beard (figure 4).

Christmas tomten, figure 4

Recipe: Rice Porridge

The last thing you need on Christmas Eve is a complicated dish to prepare, so this one is easy. You can even use the left-over rice from the Chinese food you ordered while you were busy making tomtens. This recipe makes enough for four humans and one household sprite.

Ingredients:

- 2 cups cold cooked white rice
- 2½ cups whole milk
- ½ cup sugar
- ½ cup ground almonds
- Dash vanilla extract
- Dash sherry (optional unless you are cooking for a Danish nisse, in which case you should make it a generous dash)
- Cinnamon
- Butter

Combine all ingredients except cinnamon and butter in a large pot. Stir together and heat to boiling, watching to make sure it doesn't boil over. Simmer on a low flame for 15 minutes, stirring only occasionally. Pour into a large bowl or individual dessert dishes and top with cinnamon and a pat of butter.

So You Want to Buy a Troll

Well, why not? They're awfully cute these days with their big feet, bigger noses, beady little eyes, and shaggy manes of hair. But before you pick one up at the Christmas market, you ought to know a little about its ancestry. If the troll and the helpful little Scandinavian household sprite are blood relatives, the household sprite certainly never speaks of it, while the troll is barely capable of speech. Scandinavian trolls, or "goblins" as their name is sometimes translated, do many of the things that elves and fairies do elsewhere: they keep a few cows, pilfer food from the nearby farms, and swap their own offspring for human babies.

Because they are not above stealing, many trolls are fabulously rich, though this has done nothing for their looks. They are governed by a king, but his court in Sweden is hardly a center of culture. Trolls have few practical skills. The textile arts are quite beyond them, and they have never attempted farming. They can, however, work magic and have been doing so for as long as anyone can remember. The trolls are descended from the Norse *jotnar* and *risir*, or "giants" who were present at the world's beginning, though the giants were both larger and more attractive than their great-grandchildren. They also had a bigger role to play in world events, while many of today's trolls are reduced to skulking under bridges.

One thing that can be said for the trolls is this: they are excellent timekeepers. There have been several instances in Norway and Iceland when the humans lost count of the dark days of winter and had to ask the trolls when to celebrate Christmas. Since trolls are illiterate, they probably used the old Norwegian *primstav,* a sort of farmer's almanac inscribed on a yardstick. Yule was marked by the image of an ornately carved drinking horn. As far as we know, the trolls, like us, have now made the switch from the Julian to the Gregorian calendar.

The trolls are most likely to be about on Christmas Eve, perhaps so they can admire one another's treasure hoards. This is the one night of the year that humans can take a peek at the trolls' subterranean lairs, for the hills rise up on golden pillars to reveal the glittering heaps of chalices, coins, and candelabra. The trolls are hoarders *par excellence*, never pawning or selling any of their loot no matter how hard times get.

Because they're such terrible cooks, and too stingy to order in, trolls are always glad of a free meal on Christmas Eve. If you want to prepare dinner for a troll, you must include a generous helping of meat. A few trolls, having converted to Christianity, promised they would no longer eat human flesh, but you can hardly expect them to be vegetarians. Leave the troll's meal out in the woods, far from the house; you don't want him peering in the window when you open your Christmas presents.

If you decide to take things a step further and install a troll inside your home, keep him out of the kitchen. He has an aversion to iron, so your stainless-steel kitchen implements are sure to put him off. And whatever you do, don't put him in the window; the sunlight will either turn him to stone or cause him to explode. Keep your troll in a dark, out-of-the-way corner, and all should be well. If you notice any coins, jewelry, or candlesticks going missing, you'll know just where to look. If he does explode, don't expect your household sprite to clean up the mess. If, however, your troll accidentally turns to stone, you can always move him to the garden.

CHAPTER SEVEN

Reindeer Games

We know that Santa Claus took his name, if not his character, from the fourth-century St. Nicholas, Bishop of Myra in Asia Minor. His headquarters, therefore, really ought to be in Turkey, perhaps among the outbuildings of some crumbling mountain monastery. There, elves bearded and hooded like orthodox monks would whittle away by the light of the beeswax candles, all the while conversing quietly in New Testament Greek. Under the smudged gaze of the icons, they would keep themselves busy boxing up batches of Turkish delight to distribute to the world's children. Or, Santa might have placed his enterprise further to the east, amid the snows of Mount Ararat, where the wrecked stalls of Noah's ark would be put to good use again as workshops and warehouses. What better setting for the elves as they carve all those toy animals?

If I were to posit a third location for Santa's workshop, it would have to be the federal state of Thuringia in east-central Germany. *Das Wütende Heer*, as the Wild Hunt was known in the snow-covered Thuringian forest, was led by a white-bearded gentleman named Eckhard. The Hörselberg, the magical mountain from which the procession issued, belonged to a goddess referred to in the thirteenth-century *Tannhäuser* legend as Venus, Roman goddess of love, but who might originally have been Freya, one of the Vanir, or Norse fertility gods. The errand on which Eckhard and his troop were bound was a trip around the world, an excursion that took them only five hours. Unfortunately, no sleigh is mentioned in relation to Eckhard, only a black horse and a staff. And since the Hörselberg, a.k.a. "Venusberg," was the scene of fertility-inducing sexual license, the elves would probably have been making the wrong sort of toys.

Like St. Martin's Land, Santa's realm is necessarily one of the imagination, and for various reasons the Arctic serves as the most magical blueprint for this never-to-be-discovered country. But before we can explore the reasons why, we must explore a name. Lapland, which lies well within the frozen embrace of the Arctic Circle, is so called because it is the home of the Lapps, a non-Germanic Scandinavian people who have been there for as long as anyone can remember.[24] Although they share certain aspects of their culture with the peoples of Siberia, their language is most closely related to Finnish. The term *Lapp* is so old that its etymology is uncertain. One theory is that "Lapp" meant "patch of cloth": not such a strong

24. Because of their stature, smaller than that of their Russian or Germanic neighbors, and because of their supposedly peculiar cranial measurements—early-twentieth-century anthropologists were wild for cranial measurements—the Lapps, like Gardner's pixyish Picts, have also been put forward as the original elves.

indictment, especially given that it may simply refer to the use of appliqué in their traditional woolen garments. Then again, it may come from a Finnish word meaning "people who live at the edge of the world." The Norwegians referred to them not as Lapps but as "Finns on skis." Either way, the preferred term is now *Sami*,[25] which is what the Sami have been calling themselves all along, so that is the term I will use.

When it comes to their homeland, I am going to stick with "Lapland," because, at least for us non-Sami, "Lapland" says Christmas magic far better than the more-correct *Sápmi*. Lapland's reputation as a magical place inhabited by a magical people probably goes all the way back to the first encounters between Norsemen and Sami. Even before the divisive advent of Christianity, the Sami differed from their Nordic neighbors both culturally and spiritually. While their southern neighbors were able to scratch out a few farms from the deciduous forests and the steep banks of the fjords, the Sami's arctic environment dictated nomadism. The word *tundra* comes from Sami. During the blink-of-an-eye summer, the surface of the tundra turns into a spongy, insect-ridden bog. The rest of the year, it is covered in ice and snow. And while the mountains of Lapland are picturesque, they are impossible to farm. The only crop the Sami could depend on was lichen, the reindeer's mainstay.

For the Sami, the spirits of the mountains and bogs were always close at hand. The Sami gods were visible in such naturally occurring idols as an oddly shaped boulder or birch snag, and they were audible through the medium

25. You will also find it spelled "Same" and "Saami."

of the reindeer-skin drum. In both the pagan and the early Christian eras, the Norsemen, whose native religion was shamanic to a somewhat lesser degree, often employed the Sami as consultants in times of supernatural need. With the help of the drum, the *noide*, or Sami shaman, allowed his spirit to fare forth from his body, enabling it to spy on people and find lost objects in places as far away as Iceland.

The Sami's reputation as a magical people endured over distance and through time. The Norse sagas tell of children like Gunhild Asursdatter, who was sent away to learn witchcraft from two men of Finmark, one of the northernmost portions of Lapland. These men were such powerful sorcerers that they could kill with a glance.[26] In Russia, Ivan the Terrible sent an envoy to the Sami to get their take on the recent appearance of a comet. It was believed that the Sami could also raise thunder and lightning and control the winds by the tying and untying of knots. In 1844, Andersen's "The Snow Queen" featured a Wise-woman of Finmark who could "twist all the winds of the world into a rope."

While the Catholic Church frowned upon such doings, it was the Lutherans, still caught up in the zeal of the Reformation, who really got the persecutions going. Suffice it to say that we are lucky to have any of the noide's old drums left to look at. But the flame of magic, even the smoky rumor of magic, is a hard one to snuff out. No matter how thick a layer of ashes you kick over it, the fire always struggles back to life,

26. Gunhild eventually becomes a witch in her own right, but she repays her teachers very poorly. She charms them to sleep and cinches them up in sealskin bags into which she invites King Harald Hairfair's men to thrust their weapons.

though it may not burn the same color as before. The Sami retained their supernatural aura well into the nineteenth century—long enough to sell the jolly old elf eight head of tiny flying reindeer.

All of this is most likely unknown to the average letter-to-Santa-writer. Still, the old man's arctic idyll persists. Perhaps it has something to do with Lapland itself. Most of us have witnessed snow's power to transform an ordinary landscape into a white wonderland. Now add to this the lambent play of the aurora borealis, the "blue lights" that the Snow Queen burns in her palace each evening. Behind these blowing veils, the stars show crisp and clear, while the moon admires her reflection in the hard crust of the snow. And then there are the acoustic qualities of snow. Compare the steady jingle of a reindeer's harness ringing out over the frozen tundra to the hollow clanging of a goat's bell in the dry Turkish hills.

Whatever the source of Lapland's magic, it's too late for Santa to relocate. Following the lead of dear Virginia's rule of thumb, "If you see it in the *Sun*, it's so," children's program host Markus Rautio announced on Finnish radio in 1927 that Joulupukki, the Finnish Father Christmas, made his home on Lapland's three-peaked Korvatunturi Fell. Because it straddles the border between Russia and Finland, the mountain is off-limits to the casual visitor. In this respect, English-language media has gone one better, convincing children that Santa's workshop is planted squarely at the North Pole. Theoretically at least, one could get permission from the border patrol to climb Korvatunturi Fell, but the North Pole? I suspect that the "Santa lives in Lapland" theory has been actively suppressed in the United States because we don't want our children getting wind of the fact that there is now a sort of Finnic Disney World near Lapland's capital, Rovaniemi. There, you can meet Joulupukki himself, observe the elves at work, and ride in a sleigh drawn by reindeer, all for the price of a transatlantic plane ticket plus hotel.[27]

Stallo

Yule has never loomed particularly large on the Sami calendar. Their reluctance to celebrate the birth of Christ is reflected in the laws enacted in the eighteenth century requiring church attendance on December 24. Well into the twentieth century, the holiday, for many Sami, paled in comparison to Easter or St. Andrew's Day (November 30). There were, however, special precautions to be taken on Christmas Eve. Sami parents warned their children to be on their best behavior as preparations were made for the arrival of a certain sleigh. Firewood was stacked neatly, so the sleigh's runners would not snag on any out-sticking twigs, and a sturdy branch was staked by the river so the driver could tie up his vehicle and drink his fill of the cold water before moving on. Move on quickly was what the Sami were anxious for him to do, for this driver was not Santa but a wicked giant named Stallo.

Stallo resembles the troll of Swedish fairy tale, with a huge nose, tiny eyes, and knotted black hair. Some say he is as stupid as a troll, while in other accounts he has magical

27. If you're not up for this kind of adventure, you can put your kids off the scent by showing them the Finnish film *Rare Exports: A Christmas Tale*, which builds on the Korvatunturi Fell theory but features a Joulupukki they won't *ever* want to meet.

abilities comparable to those of the noide. Stallo is actually only half troll; the other half is human. This human half may link him to the early Samis' conception of their non-Sami neighbors, or at least to their dead. The material culture of the Sami was founded on wood, skin, and bone, while Stallo was greedy for silver and gold. The ancient reindeer herders could not have failed to notice their more settled neighbors' devotion to metallurgy, an apparently magical process, or the value they placed upon its incorruptible products. This is not to suggest that the Sami were naïve; within the mythologies of the metallurgists themselves, the smith is portrayed more as a magician or god than as an ordinary craftsman—the smith Ilmarinen of the Finnish epic *Kalevala* forged the lids of heaven, among other wonders, and the Anglo-Saxon Wayland the Smith bears the epithet "lord of the elves."

Stallo continues to be associated with non-Sami graves and stone house foundations within Lapland: that is, with those places haunted by the ghosts of Norse or Finnish settlers. Perhaps a band of Sami had witnessed the laying in howe of some Bronze or early Iron Age warrior all clad in armor, his sword at his side. Before such a grave was eventually abandoned, they would have observed the leaving of offerings on the grave mound and concluded that the clanking ghost within must be propitiated or at the very least avoided. Stallo's name may come from a word meaning "metal," and he does love the stuff. In one story, he falls through a hole in the ice because his eyes are fixed upon the moon, which, he is convinced, is made of gold. In another, he is weighed down by a haul of silver, though it is usually children he lugs around in his sack.

The fact that Stallo prefers to cook children before he eats them usually gives them a chance to outwit the brute, make their escape, and count it as a lesson learned. Because he only snatches naughty children, he appears to be in the same class as Čert and Black Peter. While those two labor under the restraining influence of St. Nicholas, Stallo would not think twice about stuffing good girls and boys in his sack. But he can only ever get his hands on the bad ones. It is the children who disobey their parents—staying out too late is the most common offense—who find themselves en route to Stallo's cauldron. Stallo, then, is a cautionary figure, and not all Stallo stories end happily.

It's one thing to pretend you can't hear your mother calling because you're too busy trying out your new pair of skis in the moonlight, or to take your time coming home from your friend's *kota* on a bright summer evening, but once upon a time there were some really horrible children in Lapland: three boys who refused to accompany their parents to church on Christmas Eve. Unlike the virtuous little red-socked children in "See My Grey Foot Dangle," these boys are plotting mischief as soon as they shut the door behind their mother and father. Instead of staying safe inside the house[28] as they were told, they venture outside to try their hands at slaughtering a reindeer.

Unfortunately, there are no reindeer to be found, so the youngest boy agrees to play the part of the sacrifice. He may have thought his brothers were only playing a game, but soon his blood stains the snow. The other two hack him to

28. Even those Sami who are still nomadic maintain villages of permanent houses where they spend much of the winter.

pieces and light the fire under the pot. As the meat cooks, the smell of human flesh draws Stallo from the forest. In an instant, he is upon the surviving brothers, his huge head and tangled hair blotting out the stars. The first boy is killed instantly, while the second escapes into the house and hides inside a chest. It is he who suffers the worst death of all, for Stallo kindles a fire inside the chest by blowing sparks through the keyhole and roasting the boy alive.

One expects such things from Stallo, but how to explain the boys' own cannibalistic behavior? Well, just as Stallo is half-troll, it was rumored that some Sami might be half-Stallo, for the monster had a huge sexual appetite as well. In many of the tales he is either happily or unhappily married to a troll woman, but he prefers the pretty young Sami girls. In Finland, the Christmas processions of earlier centuries sometimes included a randy Stallo: a large youth dressed in ragged black clothing who tried to poke his wooden club up the girls' skirts. (This may be the reason why so many Finnish girls now go about dressed as male or at least asexual tonttu at Christmastime.) So perhaps the boys were Stallo's progeny.

Then again, maybe the boys weren't really so bad after all. They may simply have been re-enacting a Christmas ritual they had seen their elders perform—with a real reindeer rather than a human child. Too young to understand what they were doing, though not to get the job done, they might have expected their little brother to be returned to them on the tide of the northern lights, which some Sami believe to be a manifestation of the ancestors.

The Yuletide People

It is not entirely clear who or what the Yuletide People were, though they appear to be part of the widespread northern tradition of honoring and feasting the dead at this time of year. We know that they were the recipients of sacrifice and that the air was thick with them on Christmas Eve. We do not know what they looked like or how much sympathy they might have had for humankind. What we do know comes from scenes painted on drums as well as from the complaints of seventeenth-century clergymen. At least one Protestant cleric referred to these Sami spirits as the *Julheer*, linking them, at least in the mind of the writer, with *Das Wütende Heer* and with the *Jolorei*, yet another name for the Norse Yule Host or Wild Hunt. But it was a German theologian's *Juhlavolker*, translated poetically into English as "Yuletide People,"[29] that has stuck.[30]

Try as they might to get the Sami to Mass, those harried clergymen could not prevent some of their parishioners from slipping outside to attend older spirits, for the Sami gods were not to be found inside a church. One of the ceremonies involved removing all but the trunk and central

---

29. The furthest back that I have been able to trace the English term *Yuletide People* is 1954, when it is offered as translation of both *joulu-herrar* and *joulu-gadze*. It appears in the essay "The Lapps and Their Christmas," by Ernst Manker in the book *Swedish Christmas*. On the book's copyright page, translations are attributed to "Mrs. Yvonne Aboav-Elmquist, M. A. Oxford, and others."

30. "Stuck where?" you might ask if you are hearing the term for the first time. Surprisingly enough, the subject of the Yuletide People was a popular seasonal filler in smaller American newspapers of the 1970s.

boughs of what would today be a modest-sized Christmas tree. A reindeer was then slaughtered and the tree painted with its blood. Select portions of the sacrifice, including the lips, were draped over the branches and consecrated to the Yuletide People.

In yet another ritual, the participants fasted, collecting morsels of their Christmas Eve feast in a boat-shaped birch-bark basket painted red, again with reindeer blood, and sealed with melted fat. The basket was then hung from a tree in the forest, too high up for wolves or naughty children to pull down. Only after this spiritual Christmas hamper had been delivered could the mortals return home to their own festivities.

I do not know if it is possible to draw the Yuletide People into your own observance without blood, molten fat, and fresh reindeer lips, but you can certainly try. Pack a basket full of Christmas goodies and consecrate it to the Yuletide People but donate it to the living. You can also take note of the role of the *seite* in ancient Sami religion. A seite is an unusually shaped feature of the landscape such as a rock or a tree stump. A carving knife was sometimes used to tease out a figure that nature had already suggested, but for the most part a seite is found, not made. The seite was deemed worthy of sacrifice, and not all sacrifices were bloody. Although the gods did occasionally call out through the drum for the gift of a horse or a reindeer, bones, coins, and all manner of trinkets could also be offered to the seite.

On, Prancer!

Thanks to the names given them by Clement Moore, not to mention the work of Arthur Rankin and Jules Bass, we tend to think of the eight tiny reindeer pulling Santa's sleigh as males, but the females of *Rangifer tarandus* also sport modest antlers with which they protect their calves from potential predators. Reindeer calves are conceived in September and born in May, so the does are already a few months gone by Christmas Eve. I doubt Santa would want to endanger the health of a gestating female by asking her to pull a fully loaded sleigh around the globe, so Dasher, Dancer, and all the rest are probably males.

They cannot, however, be bulls, for all that autumnal rutting has left the mature, sexually potent males too weak to pull the sleigh. The exhaustion following the frenzy of courtship shows itself in the bulls' antlers, which by early winter have begun to drop off. And when did you ever see one of Santa's reindeer with only half a rack?

There is only one kind of reindeer suitable for pulling Santa's sleigh and that is the *harke*, or castrated male. The harke, whose testicles were traditionally bitten off by the herdsman, is real Christmas-card material. With few demands on his energy, he is able to keep his fine antlers as well as a thick coat and enough body fat to keep him going on his world tour. A harke in harness looks very festive indeed, for the old-time reindeer harness is an elaborate affair, the leather collar adorned with appliqué, couched tin thread, and a variety of bells.

The Witch's Drum

Compared to the harke in full regalia, the reindeer in the following craft is a bit of a Plain Jim. That's because he was inspired by the many reindeer one can see painted on the Sami shaman's drum, sometimes known as a "magic drum" or even a "witch's drum." As large as a small child and roughly oval in shape, the skin of the drum was smoked to a snowy whiteness, then painted all over with figures drawn in the artist's saliva, which was made red by the chewing of alder bark. There are anthropomorphic figures, mountains, bodies of water, birds, and animals, but most of all reindeer. The edge of the drum was hung with amulets made from fur, hooves, and bone.

One of the purposes of this drum was to divine the future. When the noide had entered his trance, he placed an *arpa*, a triangular piece of metal or bone (not unlike the planchette from a Ouija board), upon the drum skin. Then he struck the drum with a stick shaped like a Thor's hammer. The arpa would then jump about from picture to picture, giving the drummer an idea of what to expect in the coming season. Sometimes, the gods spoke through the drum to request a sacrifice.

We hear quite a bit about these "witches' drums" in the Norse sagas and again in the seventeenth century when Protestant proselytizers took an interest in burning them. Since they were made of organic material, it's impossible to say how long such painted drums had been in use, but Stone Age pictures of reindeer similar to those seen on the drums have been found in red ochre on sheltered rock faces throughout Lapland.

 Craft: Sacrificial Reindeer Ornament

For this craft, I have suggested a red ribbon in token of the blood that was offered to the Yuletide People in ancient days, but it need not be a plain red ribbon. The Sami are famous for their brightly colored tablet-woven bands that often incorporate metallic thread, so don't be afraid to be festive.

Tools and materials:

2 squares white felt
Clear tape
Scissors
Needle and white thread
5 or 6 cotton balls
Toothpick
¼-inch-wide red cloth ribbon, about 6 inches long

For easier stuffing and sewing, I suggest photocopying the template (figure 1) at 129 percent. Trace and cut out your template, then stick it to your felt with a generous number of clear tape strips. This beats tracing the image onto the felt, which is more work and would leave pen marks on your finished product.

Cut out the antlers first, since they are the most intricate. When you have cut out two reindeer this way, lay them one atop the other, making sure all the details line up, and whip-stitch them together. Stitch the antlers first.

Sacrificial reindeer ornament, figure 1

Stuff the figure with wisps of cotton ball as you go. Use a toothpick to help push the stuffing in. The points of the antlers will be too skinny to stuff.

Don't forget to add the ribbon. Fold it in half and insert it in the reindeer's back and whip-stitch right through it.

Hang your finished reindeer on your Christmas tree or one dedicated to the Yuletide People.

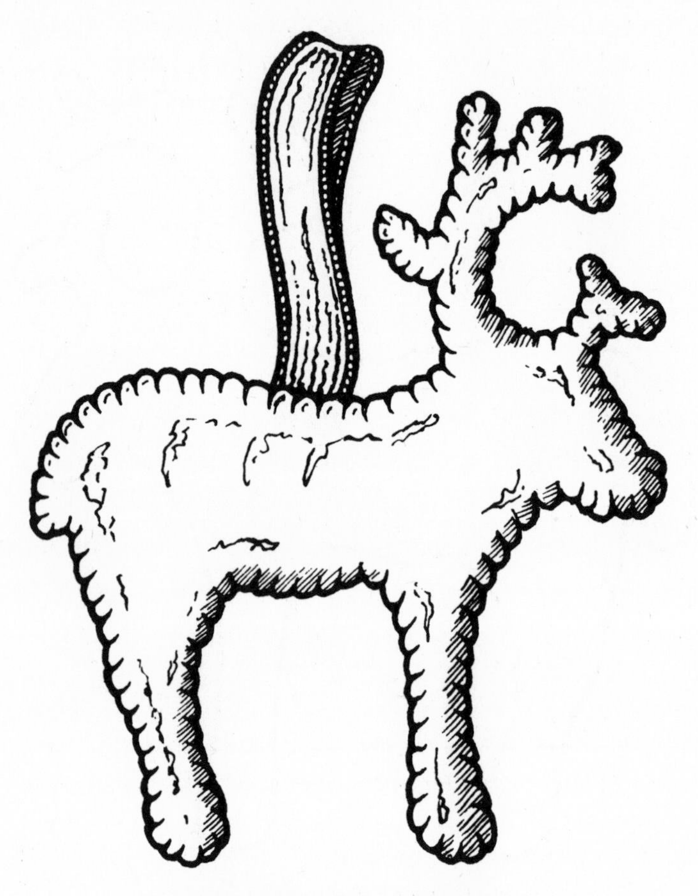

Sacrificial reindeer ornament

The Horns of Abbots Bromley

Until about 1660, reindeer were an integral part of the Christmas season in the Staffordshire village of Abbots Bromley. Since then, the Abbots Bromley Horn Dance has been held in early September, but in the late sixteenth century it was performed at New Year's and Epiphany. At that time, and possibly earlier, the six pairs of antlers were set in carved wooden heads—three painted red, three white: the heraldic colors of the village's most prominent families. The colors have since changed, but, when not in use, the antlers are still kept in St. Nicholas Church.

The dance takes place outside hallowed ground. The Deer Men, as they are called, are not the only participants in this dance, but they are certainly the main attraction. They do not actually wear the antlers, but hold the sticks with the wooden heads at chest level while supporting the weight of the antlers on their shoulders. In *The Lost Gods of England*, Brian Branston relates the Horn Dance to an incident in 1255 in which a company of thirteen cheeky poachers mounted a stag's head on a pole in the middle of Rockingham Forest in apparent mockery of the king. Branston goes on to ask the reader if it is too much to believe that in both cases the participants were acting as shamans in a once-widespread prehistoric tradition. The fact that the Abbots Bromley horns are reindeer antlers would suggest that it is not, since reindeer have been extinct in England for thousands of years. Unfortunately for Branston, the antlers were not actually handed down from the Age of the Cave Painters. They are, however, quite old, having been carbon-dated to the eleventh century, at which time they belonged to six castrated males—exactly the kind of reindeer that might be expected to pull Santa's sleigh. Even if one were to dispute the dating, England's Ice Age hunters never domesticated the reindeer and therefore would not have been in a position to castrate any of them.

The Abbots Bromley antlers must have been acquired through trade or as part of some unusual dowry. Most likely, Staffordshire was not their first stop on their way down from Lapland. Had they still been attached to the skulls, they might very well have ended up in some hunting lodge in Needwood Forest, but free-floating reindeer antlers have little commercial value unless one plans to carve them into combs, buttons, or cup handles. Whoever installed them at Abbots Bromley would have been a connoisseur of the unusual, or he was in his cups when he bought them. I would not be at all surprised if they had been won in a card game.

Another theory goes that they were brought to town by a settler from Norway. White and red are, after all, the traditional Scandinavian Yule colors. Is it too much to believe that the same settler commissioned the first seasonal Horn Dance to remind him of his homeland? No doubt it is. Nowadays, the heads are painted white and brown, not because there are no more Norwegians in the village but because those prominent families of the sixteenth century have dwindled into oblivion.

The earliest written record of the horns' appearance in what was then known as the Abbots Bromley Hobby-horse Dance dates to around 1630. The dance itself was already mentioned in 1532, but we cannot be sure the horns were part of it. As elsewhere in England, a hobby-horse remains the central figure in the dance, though most people now come to see the horns. And that is exactly why the Abbots Bromley dancers would have incorporated them into their ritual in the first place: because they had them, and the other Midlands villages did not. The purpose of the performance is clearly described in the account from the seventeenth century: to solicit monetary donations that went to spruce up the church and provide cakes and ale for the poor.

Happily, these details meant little to the folklorists who first poked their noses and their pens into the histories of such village traditions. To them, as to the later Branston, the horns and the dancers in their gaily patterned breeches were relics of Europe's long shamanic winter. Such a captivating idea is hard to dispel. Eric Maple, writing in 1977, a full twenty years after Branston, refers to the Horn Dance as "Another survival from ancient times."[31] Maple, who regards the performance as a fertility rite, reckons that the Deer Men's overriding mission is to carry blessings to the fields.

In the end, whoever hauled the six pairs of antlers into town all those centuries ago should now be hailed as a hero, for while hundreds of other hobby-horse dances have bitten the dust, the Horn Dance is still going strong. And though they probably weren't expecting it, it appears that the good citizens of Abbots Bromley have received a lasting gift from the Yuletide People.

31. See Eric Maple, *Supernatural England*, pages 41–42. While Maple's telegrammatic style can be a time-saver, I recommend Ronald Hutton's *The Stations of the Sun*, pages 90–91, for a more sober treatment of the subject.

CHAPTER EIGHT

A Christmas Bestiary

A bestiary was a book of animals: not a catalogue of accurate descriptions, but a flight of medieval fancy in which the reader was supposed to draw Christian lessons from the habits and aspects of all sorts of creatures, from lions to roosters to mermaids. There is no such moralizing in this chapter, though there is plenty of fancy. The fancies are not mine but those of our ancestors who, unlike the clerical bestiary author locked in his scriptorium, all had up-close, personal encounters with the animals in question: the horse, the goat, the pig or boar, the cat, the wolf, and the dog.

The names of four of these creatures—I suppose you could call them monsters—are preceded by the word *Yule*. In the case of the Yule Buck and Yule Cat, these are direct translations from the various Scandinavian languages. I use the names "Yule Horse" and "Yule Boar" as generic terms encompassing a variety of costumes, characters, and phenomena. Of the four, the Yule Boar is certainly the most confounding, for within the tradition we find not just a spectral Christmas pig but also a boar-shaped loaf of bread (or marzipan) and the unquiet ghost of a child. One might not immediately associate the spectral dog or the werewolf with Christmas, but they each once held a place therein, back in the days when the streets were not yet festooned with lights during the Twelve Nights of Christmas and one could never be sure what moved among the shadows.

Medieval bestiaries were often elaborately illuminated. As you read, you might wish to imagine the Black Dog chasing the grizzled Yule Cat round an ornamental capital or the *Lair Bhan* cropping the grass in the margin. You might want to hold the book at arm's length when you arrive at the Whisht Hounds, and do not be surprised if the sparks thrown from the *Gloso*'s bristling back burn a few holes in the parchment.

The Yule Horse

Had Hansel and Gretel ventured into the forest surrounding the Ilsenstein at Christmastime instead of at Midsummer, as they do in nineteenth-century composer Engelbert Humperdinck's opera, they might have run into the *Habersack*. As Yuletide horse get-ups go, the Habersack is one of the easiest to make. All you need is a broom, a forked branch to hold the bristled end up, and a white sheet to hide under. Since the effect is more that of a horned beast than a horse, the north German Habersack may originally have been a goat like the Scandinavian Yule Buck. In Yorkshire, no Christmas used to be complete without a ram, namely, the Old Derby Tup, while not far away, chimerical Oosers and Woosets stalked the moors, walking upright and wearing both beards and antlers. But the most enduring Christmas animal disguise is the horse.

Hobi in Old French is a robust little horse. A hobby-horse is a carved wooden horse's head set on a wooden frame covered by a cloth or caparison. It is indeed smaller than the average, real-life horse. The "rider" stands inside the framework so that he appears to be mounted on the horse. There is really nothing ghostly, or Christmassy, about the hobby-horse. The Elizabethans included it in their Yuletide frivolities simply because it was so very festive, but they also enjoyed it at other times of the year. Because he was in such demand, and because hobbying required special skills—the swerve the dart, the lunge—a fellow could actually make a living as a professional hobby-horse. But the hobby-horse is just one element of a public festival or, as in Elizabethan times, a lavish private pageant. Most hobby-horses now come out only in May and September.

There is another more primitive sort of horse that makes the rounds at Christmastime. It goes by many names in many different places, but these regional variations all have a few things in common. First of all, each consists of some representation of a horse's head mounted on a broomstick or other long pole. Viking re-enactors will be reminded of the scorn-pole, a horse's head and hide staked on a pole, which was used both as a public insult and to effect curses. Since its domestication, the horse has been an important and often indispensable animal. Wherever and whenever there are horses, they are venerated in one way or another. The Yule Horse conveys blessings, though it may throw in an insult or two in the process.

The actor playing the Yule Horse walks upright, if a little stooped, his body entirely covered by a sheet. Unlike the hobby-horse, the Yule Horse is not usually part of a play or dance but travels with his own band of mummers. Horses will be horses, so there is often some sort of sweeper bringing up the rear. All Yule Horses expect something for their trouble, such as food, drink, or cash.

Yule horses like to clack their jaws and charge at their hosts, but the Welsh *Mari Llwyd* is the only one who ever catches anyone. The Mari Llwyd, or "Gray Mare," is an actual horse's skull, not a carved puppet's head. A white sheet may be attached to the crown of the skull or the whole skull may be "gift-wrapped" tightly in the sheet so that the lower jaw can be made to open and close. An exposed skull can also be painted black, but the sheet covering the actor is always white. Why is she called a gray mare when she is white? Horsey people refer to apparently white horses as "grays" because the skin underneath the white coat is gray. Perhaps the Mari Llwyd was *supposed* to be gray, but no self-respecting nineteenth-century Welsh housewife would have allowed her son or husband to go parading around town in a less than blindingly white sheet.

The Mari Llwyd's eyes are made of colored glass-bottle bottoms, and her mane consists of wisps of dark horsehair bound with colorful ribbons, clapper bells, rickrack, tinsel, and whatever else you can think of. No one pretends to ride the Mari Llwyd; her "handler" walks beside her. On arriving outside each house, the mare and her attendants sing a song, asking to come in. The people inside reply, in verse, through the window or cracked door. The answer is always

"No." This goes on back and forth until one side runs out of rhymes. Whichever side wins, the mare and her party always make it over the threshold, where they are offered cakes and glasses of cider. Upon departure, the mare bestows blessings for the coming year. One of her Welsh names meant "gray-beaked bird"—yet another incarnation, perhaps, of the part-avian winter goddess.

Ireland had its own *Lair Bhan*, or "white mare," which appeared at Christmas, while the Manx *Laare Vane* cantered into the parlor at the close of the New Year's Eve dinner. The Laare Vane's head was not a real horse's skull but a wooden one painted white. The Laare Vane's visit had something for everyone. First, the horse chased the girls, then the horse's attendants performed a stick dance followed by a short mummer's play that ended with the very Celtic sacrifice of a (theatrically) severed head. The program concluded with the Laare Vane's predictions for the coming year.

The Kentish Hoodening (pronounced "oodening" because the actor wears "an hood") Horse is the Anglo-Saxon version of the Yule Horse. He does not differ much from the Celtic. The head may be a real skull or a carved hollow head in which a lit candle used to be placed. Either way, the eye sockets are left empty. The head is trimmed with a woolly mane, ribbon rosettes, bells, and the like. If you prefer black, the Old Horse, who shared his territory with the ovine Old Tup, will be more to your taste. Here, the bottle-glass eyes were set in a pony's skull that had been painted a shiny black and decorated with pompoms and braided yarn. The actor was covered by black burlap or tarp and was attended by six men with blackened faces. Though he began life as a Yule Horse, the Old Horse eventually defected to Eastertide.

The Yule Horse is now an endangered species. If you want to help keep the tradition alive, start saving your old sheets, brooms, ribbons, yarn, and bits and bobs. If you are not lucky enough to live where all manner of skulls lie bleaching in the sagebrush, you can go the easier Habersack route. Add a few clear or blue battery-powered Christmas lights under the sheet for ghostly effect, and after the first few house calls, your Yule Horse will have paid for itself.

The Yule Buck

From Sanskrit to Welsh to Middle English, the word *buck*, or a variant thereof, meant "male goat" long before it was applied to a male deer. The Scandinavian terms *Julebukk* (Danish, Norwegian) and *Julbock* (Swedish) are still often translated as "Yule Buck" instead of the more modern-sounding "Christmas billy goat." Since Christian times, the goat has been identified with the Devil, perhaps because it was the mascot of the immensely popular god Thor, later demonized by the church along with the rest of the Norse pantheon. The Yule Buck, however, is older than Thor. Somewhere on the way out of its Indo-European homeland, the word *bukka* also came to describe a mischievous, horned spirit, as in the Irish *pooka*, the Baltic *puk*, Shakespeare's Puck, and, possibly, the English *spook*. This supernatural Indo-European baggage eventually made its way into Finland, where we find the goat-man-turned-Santa Claus, Joulupukki.

A silent straw Julbock is usually the first thing you see when you enter a Swedish Christmas market. As you peruse the stalls with your mug of hot spiced wine, you'll spot another and another of his genus, some small enough to fit in your hand, others big enough to fill your front window. Apart from their size, all Yule Bucks look pretty much alike these days: bundles of rye straw bound with red ribbon, the beard represented by a few bristling ears of grain, the braided horns curving back over the withers. If you decide to buy one, you'll be investing in a very old tradition indeed.

In the old days, a Julbock could also be a man dressed up as a goat in hide, horns, and shaggy goatee. Until the late nineteenth century, the goat or goat-man was the principal Christmas gift-bringer in Nordic lands. Originally, the Yule Buck came not to hand out parcels but to accept offerings from the family in return for a bountiful harvest. If no gifts were forthcoming, he would crash around the hall, stamping his hooves and threatening the children with his horns. In order to make an especially infernal impression, the old-fashioned Julbock might hold a bundle of smoldering tow between his teeth. In Usedom in northeastern Germany, the office of Yule Buck was carried out by the *Klapperbock*, a kind of Habersack with clattering jaws. The Klapperbock terrorized those children who could not recite their prayers. Although he jettisoned his shaggy coat and horns long ago in favor of Santa Claus's red-and-white faux fur, Finland's gift-giver still goes by the ancient name of Joulupukki. In the early twentieth century, he started riding a bike to speed up his rounds on Christmas Eve. Sometimes, he went by so fast that he didn't even stop but threw the presents in the door, paperboy-style.

Even if you couldn't see him, it was expected that the Yule Buck would enter the house at some point on Christmas Eve. So as not to disappoint him, Norwegian children left a shoe-full of barley grains for him under the bed. In the area of Elverum in southeastern Norway, he was believed to spend Christmas Eve prognosticating under the dinner table. He was always gone by Christmas morning, but if he left a few plump grains behind in his place, it was a sign of a good harvest to come.

Having discharged his gift-giving duties, the Yule Buck then disappeared, popping up again at Epiphany (January 6) in Norway and Denmark to trot along behind the Star Boys as they paraded through the streets singing carols and holding a paper lantern aloft to represent the Star of Bethlehem. The very latest you could expect to run into a Yule Buck was St. Knut's Day (January 13), when he came knocking once more. The "Knut Buck," or *Nuuttipukki* as he was called in Finland, might have looked like a goat, but he drank like a man, and you had better give him as much beer as he wanted if you hoped to prosper in the new year.

Before you decide that the straw Julbock you brought home from the Christmas market is completely harmless, you should know about a handful of Scandinavian tales in which he plays a principal role. In one of them, a girl attending a Christmas Eve party takes a straw goat-man, which the other guests have been throwing around in a game of keep-away, and begins to dance with it. As the clock strikes twelve, the straw figure comes to life, rustling his partner back and forth across the parlor floor to the horror of the other partygoers. By the time they realize he is no devil in disguise but the Devil himself, it is too late; the goat-man has disappeared, taking the girl with him.

The Yule Boar

In the Viking and early medieval eras, the kept pig was not much different in appearance or attitude from its cousin the wild boar. Both were regarded with great reverence, in part because of the sharpness of their tusks. A whole pig, or its head, was the centerpiece of the Nordic Yule feast, while in Lithuania, it was the task of the one left behind on Christmas Eve to make a special stew with a pig's tail sticking out of it. In Germany, too, and in the Slavic lands to the east, the pig or boar was a staple of the old Christmas feast.

Yule pork was sacred food. In Sweden, the leftover meat was salted or dried and put away until plowing time, when it was either turned into the earth or given to the plowman and horses to eat. Sometimes, the Yule Boar was actually a loaf of bread shaped like a boar, incorporating the last grains of the harvest. Both boars and pigs act as efficient living plows as they snuffle their way through the forest in search of acorns and truffles. This churning of mulch and mast into the earth is essential to its ability to support new growth, which is probably why the boar was the signature animal of the Norse fertility god Frey. Once slaughtered, a nicely fattened pig also provided much of what a household would need to get it through the winter: sausages, salt pork, tripe, and tallow for making soap and candles. Frey himself owned a gold-bristled boar that pulled him around in a cart. Though a living creature, this *Gullinbursti* had been fashioned for the god by the dwarves. Today, Gullinbursti's descendants are made of golden marzipan and sold in little cellophane bags as good luck charms at New Year's.

That takes care of the pig on top of the table; in Sweden, if you weren't careful, there might be another one underneath it. She was the *Gloso*, or "glowing sow," and if you knew what was good for you, you would leave three stalks of wheat standing in the field at harvest time as an offering to her. You might also set out a bowl of porridge and a few fish heads for her to consume as she passed by on Christmas Eve. You could see the Gloso coming from a long way off, for her eyes burned like coals and her bristling back shed sparks as she moved. If she found the offerings too paltry, she would stay on to haunt the dark space under the tablecloth throughout the Twelve Nights of Christmas.

One of the many nicknames of Frey's twin sister Freya was *Sýr*, meaning "sow." Was Sweden's glowing sow a relic of the old fertility goddess's worship? Perhaps, for the cult of a Yuletide goddess once extended far beyond the borders of Sweden, as evinced by Perchta's midwinter ramblings. Likewise, the Gloso was not the only ghostly pig trotting about at this time of year. In Switzerland, the appearance of a flying sow heralded the coming of rough winter weather. Sometimes, she and her piglets arrived on the heels of the Wild Hunt.

In the Middle Ages, there was a widespread belief that a mother who killed her own children would return in the shape of a sow, her unshriven children trailing her as little striped piglets. In Sweden, the Gloso herself was sometimes supposed to be an *utkasting*, the ghost of a baby born out of wedlock and exposed to the elements immediately after birth. In the Faeroe Islands, such an infant ghost was known as a *niðagrisur*, a "pig from below." In addition to Christmas, these restless spirits often showed up at the weddings of their mothers or more fortunate siblings to lament their tragic fates.

And then again, the glowering sow may only have been the stunned ghost of a pig who had enjoyed a choice diet and the best of care all year, only to fall to the axe just before Christmas.

The Yule Cat

The first cat to appear in the days before Christmas was the Icelandic *Jólaköttur*, or "Yule Cat," whose favorite dish was lazy human. Since there are no wild feline predators in Iceland, the Yule Cat was probably an oversized version of the bushy Norwegian forest cats that pulled the goddess Freya's wagon through the sky.

The Yule Cat began his prowl in the autumn when everyone was supposed to be doing the heavy work involved in stocking up for the long winter. First, there was the haymaking, then the slaughter of whichever animals could not be kept through the winter, after which the meat had to be smoked and stored. The rest of the sheep's wool that had been shorn in the spring had to be spun, then knitted or woven into new garments for everyone in the household.

Anyone who did not pitch in would not get his or her yearly payment of new clothes at Christmas. The maid or farmhand who was still walking around in frayed skirts or holey trousers on Christmas Day was said to "go to the Christmas Cat," because the state of their clothes marked them as a tasty meal for the *Jólaköttur*.

The Werewolf

It was once believed that children born on Christmas Day were able to see spirits. Those born on any of the Twelve Days or Nights of Christmas, however, stood a good chance of becoming werewolves. In Romania, werewolves might also be born in September, the consequence of their parents giving in to the temptations of the flesh during Advent, which, in the Middle Ages, was supposed to be a season of penitence.

"The Wolves are Running," is the ominous watchphrase in John Masefield's 1935 children's novel, *The Box of Delights*, which opens at the beginning of the school Christmas holidays. Those who speak it are not referring to *Canis lupus* but to werewolves. The Christmas werewolf may reflect a transference of the Roman Lupercalia from the ides of February to Yule. Lupercalia was the Roman Mother's Day, a feast to celebrate the she-wolf who suckled Romulus and Remus. J. K. Rowling carries on the Christmas werewolf tradition in *Harry Potter and the Half-Blood Prince*, when Remus Lupin discusses his "furry little problem" with Harry over eggnog on Christmas Eve.

At one time, this Season of the Wolf stretched all the way from Martinmas, when the Pelzmarten donned his wolf skin, through Epiphany when the Wise Men finally arrived and banished the beasts. Latvian and Lithuanian werewolves started running amok on St. Lucy's Eve (December 12), while the shaggy black *kallikantzaroi*, identified by one German scholar as Turkish werewolves, descended on southern Greek homes on Christmas Eve. Wolves, like humans, are social animals, so it should come as no surprise that werewolves like to get together for the holidays. In Baltic lands, they gathered on Christmas night to feast on rustled cattle, washing the meat down with other people's wine and beer. These werewolves were not all bad; they belonged to a brotherhood devoted to the good of the community. If you wanted their protection during the rest of the year, you looked the other way when they pinched a keg at Christmastime.

In Germany, the transformation occurred during the Twelve Days of Christmas, when the word *Wolf* was not to be uttered. The Lithuanians were of the opposite opinion: to talk of wolves at the Christmas dinner table would keep them away. And while Baltic werewolves liked to roam at night, German werewolves tended to be wolves by day and men by night, when they left their wolf-skin shirts hanging in the wardrobe.

If you are expecting to give birth during the Twelve Days of Christmas, you might ask your friends to throw you a werewolf-themed baby shower. Someday, that baby is going to be a teenager, and what could be more cool than to be able to say, "My parents thought I was going to be a werewolf."

The Spectral Dog

The Norwegians continued to be swept up by the Oskorei into the mid-nineteenth century, but in England, the Wild Hunt broke ranks much earlier. It survived on the one hand as the ghostly coach that came barreling down the village street at midnight, pulled by a team of black and often headless horses, and on the other as a pack of spectral dogs. The coach no longer has any particular relevance to Yule, but the dogs have maintained a tenuous link with the Twelve Days of Christmas.

By the 1600s, the dogs had become identified as the hunting hounds of some rash lord who persisted in hunting on the Sabbath and, as if that were not bad enough, ordered the pack to be killed and buried with him when he died. This Sabbath huntsman has since served his time in Purgatory and is now enjoying his eternal rest, but because the dogs were sacrilegiously interred in hallowed ground, they are roaming still. In some parts of England, they were said to be the souls of unbaptized babies who, like the huntsman's hounds, had no place either in the churchyard or in the afterlife. These Gabriel, Whisht, or Yeth Hounds were consistently described as coal-black with glowing eyes. Circling above the homes of the doomed, they served as a year-round death omen, but on New Year's Eve, it was a white dog you did not want to see. A few towns in England required white dogs to be kept inside—along with any red-haired women—until the danger had passed.

The Teutonic witch-goddess Berchta also sometimes traveled with a pack of hounds. Under the north German name of Holda or Holle, she led a broomstick-mounted flight of unchristened children through the night sky, especially on the twelve nights between Christmas and Epiphany. As in England, these children could also take the forms of dogs. When the goddess herself tired of her more or less human shape, she, too, might assume the appearance of a white dog.

In Mecklenburg, Germany, on Christmas and New Year's Eve, the townsfolk shut their doors against the passing of the spectral huntress Lady Gaude—another incarnation of Berchta—and her twenty-four daughters. Because these young women had loved hunting better than the prospect of salvation, they were turned into dogs and doomed to hunt until Judgment Day. Tired of having twenty-four maws to feed, their mother would shove one of them into each front door she found standing open. Once inside, the dog curled up at the fireplace and insinuated itself into the household.

If you were foolish enough to try to kill your canine houseguest, it would turn into a stone. Throw the stone as far as you could, and it would just come trotting back again at nightfall. Though indestructible, the dog had to be treated well or all sorts of bad fortune would befall the household. If, when she returned the following Christmas, Lady Gaude found a happy, stern-waving hound with its coat nicely brushed, she would bestow her blessings upon the host family. But if you really wanted to get rid of your houseguest before the year was out, you had to do something really crazy in front of it, like brew ale in an eggshell. Like the Celtic fairy changeling, the dog would be startled into making some remark in human speech. Having blown her cover, the young huntress would then be compelled to leave.

An easier way to prosper from an encounter with the Yuletide goddess was to help her get back on the road after her carriage broke down, as it always seemed to do during the Twelve Nights of Christmas. Once you had whittled and installed the replacement part, she would invite you to pick up either the wood shavings or the droppings her waiting dogs had left by the side of the road. In the morning, they would be turned into gold.

Lady Gaude and her twenty-four daughters now belong to the realm of mostly forgotten folklore, but the lone black dog is "alive" and well in England, especially in Devon, former haunt of the Whisht Hounds. (The "Yeth," or "heathen," hounds stuck to North Devon.) Going by the names of Capelthwaite,[32] Barguest, Black Shuck, or simply "the Black Dog," his appearance does not always spell doom. Nowadays, the Black Dog might warn of impending disaster, comfort a child, or accompany a lone cyclist down a dark country lane.

A Black Dog of Down St. Mary who surprised a choir boy on his way home from Christmas supper gave every appearance of knocking down the local schoolhouse, but despite the sounds of falling masonry, no damage was actually done. Mostly, the Black Dog simply appears, as it did one foggy Christmas Eve in Worcestershire in 1943. Larger than a Great Dane, with glimmering eyes, the Worcestershire Black Dog was simply trotting by without any clicking of claws on the pavement.[33]

Many of us have met with the Black Dog or "Grim" most recently in *Harry Potter and the Prisoner of Azkaban*. While the Grim of the wizarding world is still very much a death omen, the Church Grim, which was often but not invariably a dog, was supposed to prevent witches from entering

32. It was most likely the Capelthwaite that inspired Sir Arthur Conan Doyle's *The Hound of the Baskervilles*, though a headless black dog of Dartmoor has also been in the running.

33. For these and more shaggy Black Dog stories, see Graham J. McEwan's *Mystery Animals of Britain and Ireland.*

the churchyard. The Church Grim was not a volunteer; he was pressed into service when he was dispatched and buried under the gate, usually when the church's foundations were laid. In Old Norse, a *grim* is a spectre, while in Old English, *grim* can also mean "fierce, savage."[34] The Scandinavian *kirkegrim*, who was perceived as a tiny man, is probably older than the English Church Grim, who is the result of a Danish vocabulary word introduced into an Anglo-Saxon population. Since the kirkegrim resembled a small human, it seems likely that the original foundation sacrifice was a child, not a dog.

As for Sirius Black's nickname of Padfoot, it is the name by which the Black Dog is known in Staffordshire, no doubt because of its silent paws. The Black Dog is hard to mistake for an ordinary dog. In addition to its size, which has been described as that of a calf or larger, it exits by unconventional means, either disappearing in a flash of light or simply fading from view.

34. *Grima* could also mean "mask" in Old English. The Norse God Odin was nicknamed Grimr because he liked to travel incognito, but it is not certain if the Church Grim ever belonged to him.

CHAPTER NINE

Winter's Bride

If you grew up writing letters to Santa, you are probably used to a strict separation of the secular and spiritual celebrations of Christmas. Santa Claus belongs to the mailbox, the mall, the stockings, and the hearth. The Baby Jesus belongs in the church pageant and perhaps on a Christmas card or two. But a little digging into Santa's background reveals that his nickname of "Kris Kringle" is actually a corruption of the German *Christkindl*, the diminutive form of *Christkind*, the Christ Child. In parts of Europe, it is the Christ Child himself who delivers the presents and even sets up the Christmas tree. More often that not, the part of the Christkind is played by a girl, who makes no effort to look like a boy but dresses in the veil and full white skirts of a bride. And the bride, as it happens, is one of the Yuletide goddess's most enduring forms.

The Christkind

In the Czech Republic, the Christ Child is never seen; he arranges the gifts and sometimes also the tree behind closed doors, then rings a tiny bell to signal his departure. No matter how fast the children run after the sound of the bell, they won't catch even a glimpse of his bare heels as he turns the corner. In Germany, however, a highly visible *Christkind* presides over Nuremberg's Christmas Market in a pleated gold number that looks more like a cast-off from a Cecil B. DeMille set than anything a child might have worn in ancient Palestine.

The *Nürnberger* Christkind, who also sports a golden crown and long yellow ringlets, is invariably played by a teenage girl. This instance of female-to-male cross-dressing is no recent development; the earliest illustrations of the Christkind on "his" gift-giving rounds show a girl with fair, flowing hair; a white gown; and a wreath of candles on her head. The Christ Child as ethereal gift-giver can be traced back to the early seventeenth century. Though "he" would find a permanent home in both Nuremberg and Counter-Reformation Bohemia, he was born in Protestant Germany as a reaction against the Catholic cult of St. Nicholas.

The early Christkind's crown might also be made of gold paper. In Alsace, she whitened her face with flour to help conceal her identity from the neighborhood children and to effect a greater contrast between herself and her companion, the black-faced Hans Trapp, as Knecht Ruprecht was known in those parts. She carried a bell in one hand to announce their arrival.

In the very small town of Hallwil in the Seetal region of north-central Switzerland, the *Wienechts-Chindli*, or "Christmas Child," and her colorful retinue continue to make the rounds on Christmas Eve. The Wienechts-Chindli has done the Alsatian Christkind one better: she appears completely veiled, the generous layers of tulle held in place by a golden crown with tinsel streamers. In the 1800s, when the custom was more widespread throughout the Seetal, this Christmas Child, like her invisible Czech counterpart, delivered the Christmas tree to the house. Now her visit is the occasion for lighting the candles on its branches.

In her present form, the Christmas Child looks like a cross between a Western-style bride and an Afghan princess. She is usually about thirteen years old, as are her "maids," who are always six in number. You can't expect bridesmaids to wear the same thing year after year, and their costumes have undergone subtle changes over time. In the 1800s, the maids, like the Christmas Child, dressed in white, but in the first half of the twentieth century, they switched to their Sunday best. After about 1950, they started to dress all alike, and they now appear in hooded cloaks of dusty rose. They carry lanterns and baskets of presents, singing carols at each house they visit. Their faces uncovered, they act as intermediaries between the mortal children of the household and the enigmatic Christmas Child, whose only greeting is a touch of her white-gloved hand. Unlike their early modern precursors—the ghostly, buzzing *Salige Fräuleins*, or "Blessed Young Ladies," who consumed the essence of foods left out for them at night—the Christmas Child and her attendants accept no offerings in return.

Barborka

St. Barbara was a third-century Syrian Christian martyr whose feast was celebrated on December 4. In order to have absolute control over the young Barbara, her father, Dioscorus, kept her on the top floor of an ivory tower, which is why medieval artists often portrayed her hefting an ornate little replica of her prison. When Barbara converted to the Christian faith, her father hit the tower roof, pulled out his sword, and would have slain his daughter on the spot if God had not chosen that moment to split the tower in half with a bolt of lightning, allowing the girl to leap out and flee to the mountains.

Betrayed by one of the shepherds among whom she took refuge, Barbara was subsequently imprisoned, tortured, and eventually beheaded on December 4 by none other than Dioscorus. Between Barbara's capture and death, she had just enough time to work a minor horticultural miracle that is still celebrated today. When she was taken from the mountains, a twig from a cherry tree became caught in her skirts and remained there even when she was thrown in the dungeon. Barbara tended the twig in secret, as she had her Christian faith, causing it to burst into bloom in the darkness of her cell. This is the explanation given for the "Barbara branches" that young women cut on December 4 and force into bloom by Christmas Eve. These days, Germans use the blossoming *Barbarazweigen* mostly for decorative purposes.

In Bohemia, cuttings of the sour or morello cherry were fortune-telling tools. The process varied: you could simply wait and see if your branch bloomed, and if it did, you would be married within a year and a day. If there were more than one nubile girl in the household, the one whose branch bloomed first would be the first to marry. Or, you could cut several twigs and label each with the name of a different boy. The boy whose branch bloomed first was the one whom you would marry. In Czech, such a branch is known as a *Barborka* (plural, *Barborky*), or "little Barbara."

At dusk on the eve of St. Barbara's Day, a whole tribe of Barborky took to the streets. These were no twigs but actual girls. Beneath a chaplet of leaves or flowers, the Barborka was sometimes masked, sometimes veiled, but more often she simply let her long hair hang in her face. If she happened not to have an abundance of hair, or if it were a boy taking over the role, then "she" could make a wig of tow or the golden "wavy hair grass" (*Avenella flexuosa*) that grew in the meadows. Since St. Barbara died a virgin, the flowing hair may be a token of her refusal to marry the man of her father's choosing, but there the Barborka's resemblance to the martyr ends.

The Barborka was unique to central Bohemia, and her costume varied from village to village. She might wear a black dress, shoes, and stockings in keeping with the more frightful aspect of what Leopold Kretzenbacher in his 1959 work, *Santa Lucia und die Lutzelfrau*, has termed the *Mittwinter Frau*, or "Midwinter Woman," an unpleasant and unabashedly heathen figure who began putting in appearances throughout Europe at this time of year. While in black, the Barborka was more of a Midwinter Witch. Once a female leader of the Wild Hunt, this diminished goddess later went about on foot, her hair hanging down in tangles instead of streaming out behind her.

The Midwinter Witch might also be arrayed in white, and when springtime came, her number was up. In Slavic lands, she was put to death under many names: Marzana, Morena, Morana. She could be made of straw, birch, or braided hemp. The Sorbs, a Slavic minority of eastern Germany, dressed theirs in a white shirt provided by the household in which a death had most recently occurred, while the bride who had most recently been married donated her veil to complete the scarecrow's costume. After it had been ritually stoned, this "Winter's Bride" was drowned in the nearest body of water. As her broken bits passed on downstream, they took Old Man Winter with them, allowing spring to come.

But at Advent, the springtime is still a long way away. The Midwinter Witch is just finding her stride, and she will grow ever fiercer as she speeds toward her own feast day at Epiphany (January 6). Since the earliest days of the Church, efforts were made to subdue or at least to prettify the Midwinter Witch. On St. Barbara's Eve she was re-christened in honor of the martyr. She was also placed in the vanguard of Svatý Mikuláš, the Czech version of the gift-giving St. Nicholas. After the Counter-Reformation, which lasted from 1542 until 1648, the Barborka began to resemble the Christ Child, who now delivered the presents on Christmas Eve. In her heyday around the end of the nineteenth century, the Barborka wore a blue or scarlet sash atop a crisp white lace-trimmed dress under which sprouted an abundance of petticoats. The sash was tied on her left side, corresponding to her "basket hand." (In those villages where the tradition survives, white remains the color of choice for the dress, and the red sash has won out over the blue.) In Barborka's right hand, she carried a broom or wicker carpet beater.

The Barborky, who usually traveled in batches, did not ring the doorbell but struck the windows with their cleaning implements. Crossing the threshold, they announced that they had come all the way from the tiny village of Dražíč in South Bohemia to determine whether or not there were any good children in the house. If not, Barborka would swat the children with her broom or beater and let St. Nicholas know that there was no point in stopping when he passed through on the night of December 5. Good children received fruits and candies from the basket. Then, her message delivered, Barborka departed to bang on the windows of the next house.

Lucia

Yet another bridelike figure persists in the Swedish Lucia. Before the radical adjustments made to the calendar in the sixteenth century, the longest night of the year fell, or was supposed to fall, on December 13. English poet John Donne referred to St. Lucy's Day as "Both the year's and the day's deep midnight." Never a big deal in England, the feast of Santa Lucia is one of the most important celebrations of the year in Sweden, whose unique observance of the day has spread to Norway, Finland, Denmark, and the Swedish communities of North America, each of which elects its own "official" Lucia.

By the 1700s, the Swedish Lucia had started taking fashion hints from the Lutheran Christkind. Since the early twentieth century, the standard Lucia costume has been a long white dress like a nightgown, a wide red ribbon tied at the waist, and a crown of at least six white tapers set in a wreath of lingonberry sprigs, though bay or box will do as long as the greens are fresh. (A wet handkerchief stretched over the top of the head will also help prevent the spread of flames without spoiling the effect.) A chandelier-like metal crown, not unlike the traditional Nordic bridal crown, is also acceptable, as are battery-powered candles if the Lucia is very small. Early Lucias tended to wear puffier gowns, in keeping with the fashions of the times, and the sash might be blue or draped across the chest. "Lucia 1908," a painting by Carl Larsson, in which he depicts one of his daughters in what appears to be an actual nightgown, may have led to the simplified design.

The third-century St. Lucy was another virginal Christian martyr whose story does not differ much from St. Barbara's. Before her demise, St. Lucy was able to make herself useful by handing out gifts of bread to the poor, which is the reason given why Swedish household and office Lucias deliver coffee, pepper cookies, and saffron buns on the morning of December 13. Finland elected its first national Lucia in 1930, but the old Finnish stave calendar had already marked the date with the image of a candle. Despite the fact that Iceland had two churches dedicated to St. Lucy before the rest of Scandinavia had any, there were no Icelandic Lucias until 1954, and even then they were celebrated only by those Icelanders who had some connection to Sweden. In Denmark, where *Lussinatt* used to be a night of augury, the tradition dates only to 1944, the year King Christian X was taken prisoner by the Nazis and the country began to experience its own deep midnight. Dressed in white, with crowns of tinsel or lighted candles, the Danish Lucias appear on the night of the twelfth rather than the morning of the thirteenth as in Sweden. On this erstwhile darkest night of the year, it is the Danish Lucias' mission to bring a little sparkle to nursing homes, hospitals, and wherever else there is a desperate need to dispel winter's gloom.

There are plenty of supporting roles in a Swedish Lucia procession. Lucia's maids carry candles while star boys wear tall, pointed hats adorned with foil stars and sing their own set of songs in addition to the obligatory "Santa Lucia." There may even be a few Christmas elves bearing lanterns. Since 2008, boys have been fighting for the right to wear their schools' Lucia crowns, and girls to act as star boys, both with limited success.[35] In response to those who insist that Lucia must be a girl with flowing blond hair, I would point to the old-fashioned "Lussi-boys," university students who strolled around singing carols to earn their Christmas pocket money, and to the now-vanished West Gotland practice of placing the candle crown on the farm's best cow.

According to legend, the first "Lussi," as she was known in earlier times, was a local girl who appeared in the pre-dawn hours of a winter's morning to deliver food to the starving villagers of western Sweden. These days, she shows up with a coffeepot and a basket of saffron buns, or *Lussekatter*. These "Lussi cats" may point to the Norse fertility goddess, Freya, whose chariot was pulled by cats. Unfortunately, there is no

35. See "Boys blocked from bearing 'girls-only' Lucia crown" at http://www.thelocal.se/16308/20081212/ (*The Local: Sweden's News in English*, December 12, 2008).

record of such "cat buns" before 1620, at which time they were baked for St. Nicholas Day in the sometimes-German, sometimes-Danish province of Holstein.

Recipe: Lussekatter

These buns come in a wide variety of traditional shapes, bearing such imaginative names as Goat Cart, Peacock, and Priest's Hair. The general name by which they are known is *Lussekatter*, meaning "Lucy cats." The most common shape is the "S" scroll presented here, which many Swedes identify as the Cat itself. Others call it the boar or simply the Twist. Two "C" scrolls placed back to back might also be the Cat or a set of Wagon Wheels. Because they're labor intensive, Lussekatter can be made ahead of time, frozen, and warmed in the oven before the sun comes up on December 13. Serve them with coffee and candlelight.

Ingredients:

- ½ cup (1 stick) unsalted butter, plus a little more for greasing
- 1 cup whole milk
- 1 goodly pinch saffron threads
- 5 cardamom pods or ½ teaspoon ground cardamom (both optional)
- ½ cup sugar, plus a little more for sprinkling
- 1 package active dry yeast
- 2 eggs, beaten, plus 1 egg white for glaze
- 4–4½ cups white flour
- ⅓ cup dried currants

Put the stick of butter in a small pot with the milk and heat on low just until the butter is melted. While you are waiting, crumble the saffron threads between your fingers or grind them in a small mortar and pestle, then add them to the butter/milk mixture and let stand. Split open your cardamom pods, if you are using them, and let the dark seeds drop into the mortar. Crush. (No need to wash the mortar and pestle in between the saffron and the cardamom.) Mix the crushed cardamom seeds, sugar, yeast, and 1 cup flour in a large bowl. Gradually stir in the warm saffron mixture. Add beaten eggs and the rest of the flour a little at a time.

On a floured surface, knead the dough for about 10 minutes. Shape into a ball and place in a large, butter-smeared bowl. Cover with a damp towel and leave in a warm place to rise for about 45 minutes. Punch the dough down and turn onto a lightly floured surface. Cover with the towel and let rest about 5 minutes.

In the meantime, soak the currants in a bowl with hot water. After 5 minutes, drain currants and set aside.

Pinch off a piece of dough to make a ball slightly larger than a golf ball. Roll it into a rope between your hands and shape into an "S" scroll or, if you prefer, make a slightly more realistic cat's head by flattening a small ball for the cat's face, then pinching two smaller balls into ears. Place buns on a greased or foil-lined cookie sheet.

Cover your first sheet of buns with the damp towel and let rise about 10 minutes while you prepare the second sheet.

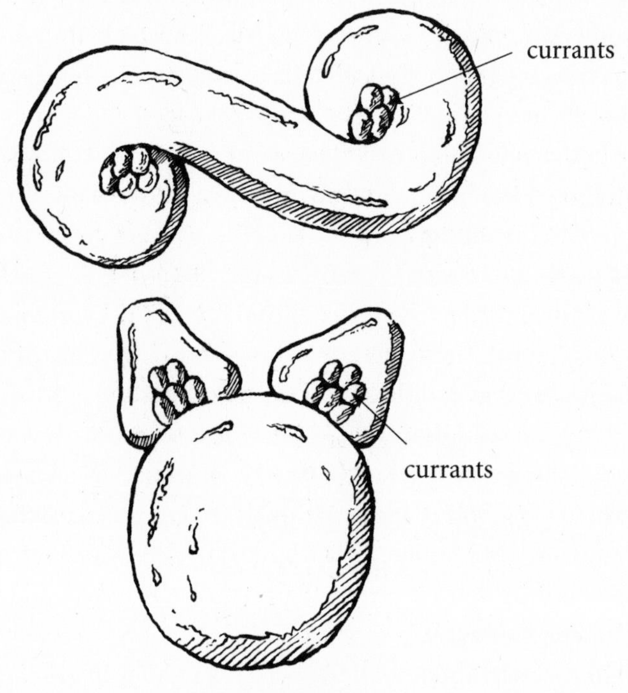

Lussekatter

Just before you put your buns in the oven, brush them with a beaten egg white and firmly press dried currants into dough for accents. Sprinkle buns with sugar and bake at 375°F for 10–15 minutes.

Night Walks with Heavy Steps

Like Denmark, Norway adopted the modern Lucia procession during World War II, thereby eclipsing the distant memory of a much older, darker spirit. This Lussi or *Lussibrud* (i.e., "Lucy Bride") was the witchlike leader of the *Lussiferd*, her own special detachment of the Wild Hunt. On December 13, this troop of goblins swept down on the Norwegian farmhouses to help themselves to bread and beer. If there were any naughty children inside, Lussi herself might slip down the chimney to teach them a lesson.

"Night walks with heavy steps," opens one of several Scandinavized versions of the old Neapolitan folk song "Santa Lucia." In addition to marking the winter solstice Old Style, December 13 was also one of the medieval Ember Days, fasting days interspersed throughout the seasons to remind humankind to repent. Cookies, buns, and fish were all right, but meat was forbidden. On Ember Days, the rich were supposed to give food to the poor, just as the legendary Lucia doled out loaves from her basket. Whether the night of the full moon, solar event, cross-quarter day, or one of that handful of leftover days at the end of the year, whenever a date was designated as extraordinary, the door was left open to supernatural interference. As one of the Ember Days *and* the longest night of the year, *Lussinatt* was double trouble.

In Latvia, the werewolves came out on St. Lucy's Eve, while in Austria, as in old Norway, it was a night of witches. In the mountains, things were relatively calm, but where the land flattened out toward the Hungarian plain, it was necessary to carry a frying pan full of glowing coals and blackthorn (*Prunus spinosa*) twigs through the house to smoke out those witches and goblins that might otherwise plunder the winter stores. In southern Austria, large round pancakes were baked in the hot ashes of the fireplace—the sun goddess's wagon wheels, perhaps?—and a braided yeast bread known as a *Luziastriezel* was baked as an antidote for the bite of a rabid dog.[36] To the north and east in Burgenland, it did not matter how many pancakes you made or how thick the smoke rolling through the parlor; you could still expect a visit from the dreaded *Lutzelfrau*.

The Lutzelfrau

Known also as *Fersenlutzel*, or "Heel Lucy," because she threatened to cut out your Achilles tendon, and *Budelfrau* and *Pudelmutter*, an old mother who let presents rain down from her voluminous skirts, this witch was both disciplinarian and gift-giver in one. If you were lucky, you would never see her; she would throw her gifts in at the door, which had been mysteriously left ajar. But more often she would step inside in all her horrific glory.

Here she comes, an old peasant woman with kerchief and glowering, ash-smeared countenance. She appears completely foreign, for surely no one so ugly has ever lived in the village. She certainly looks nothing like the teenaged sister or housemaid who slipped out a little while ago and hasn't come back yet. First, this pushy old hag inspects the floors, the furniture, the cupboards, and the dishes inside them to make sure everything has been properly washed, dusted, waxed, and polished. Then she turns her attention to the children. Have they also been scrubbed? Have they been sweeping, studying, praying, obeying their parents, and get-

36. There are a handful of ancient goddesses and goddesslike figures who often appeared with dogs, among them Diana, St. Walburga, and the Lowland Nehalennia. The dogs might reflect these goddesses' early identities as huntresses or as queens of the dead, for the dog was a popular escort to the underworld. Going her own way was the fertility goddess Freya with her string of cats.

ting to bed on time? Convinced that all is in order, she finally decides against abducting any of the children.

Before she goes, she gives her skirts a shake, letting fall an abundance of sweets, fruits, and nuts interspersed with turnips and potatoes. The root vegetables are seized by the older children, who know there are sure to be coins hidden inside. As the children scramble for the prizes rolling all over the floor, the Lutzelfrau disappears. A little while later, the older sister returns—and didn't she just pass the strangest character on the way home?

Lucka

Yet another sort of Lucy haunted the formerly German-speaking areas of Bohemia. Like her Austrian counterparts, the Lucka of Neuhaus was neither young nor pretty, and underneath her skirts she was not even female. Though the Lucka, too, has taken a form of the saint's name, she is more closely related to the old goddess-cum-folk-figure, Perchta, specifically, *Schnabelpercht*, or "Beak Perchta."

The beak remained a prominent feature of the nineteenth-century Bohemian Lucka, and what a beak it was, concealing all but the piercing eyes of the impersonator, who, as a rule, was a teenaged boy. The wooden framework of the beak was covered by a white handkerchief with two eyeholes cut in it. This was knotted at the back of the neck, after which a large white kerchief was stretched over the head and tied either under the chin or on top of the head. A woman's dress and cloak completed the costume. By holding the point of the beak's framework in his mouth, the actor could make the pieces clack noisily as he inspected the house, stirring up any lingering dust on the furniture with his *Federwisch*, or "feather-wipe." This was not the ineffectual feather *duster* with which French maids flap about the house but the last joint of a goose's wing with feathers intact, yet another relic of the bird goddess.

In fact, Lucka may have had another, more mysterious reason for making sure the floors were swept clean: she did not want anyone to see what sort of footprints she left. But if there was snow on the ground, as there was sure to be during Advent in Bohemia, her splayed foot might still leave behind the pentangular *Drudenfuss*, or "Drude's foot," a sure sign that a *Drude*, or bird-woman, had passed that way. On December 13, the Drudenfuss was also a Christian talisman, for the five points of the star correspond to the five letters in the saint's Latin name, "Lucia."

Craft: Lucka Mask

Here is a paper version of the old Bohemian disguise that was made of wood splints and linen. If you think you might not have a chance to wear your Lucka mask—who has the time these days?—you can use smaller circles and make a few maskettes to hang around the house from December 12 until Christmas Eve.

Tools and materials:

- 2 large sheets watercolor or heavy drawing paper
- Dinner plate for tracing
- Cake plate or round serving platter, also for tracing
- Pencil
- Scissors
- Ruler
- Glue

X-Acto or other craft knife
Hole puncher
White yarn or ribbon
Silver glitter, Q-Tip (both optional)

Trace the dinner plate and the cake plate on the two sheets of paper to make one small and one large circle. Cut both circles out. Fold each circle into quarters and unfold. The dotted lines in figures 1 and 2 show the creases.

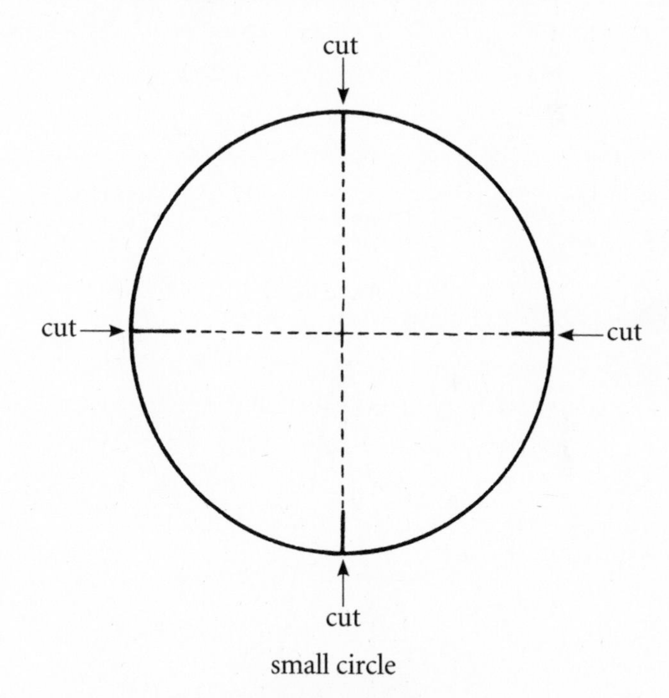

Lucka mask, figure 1

On the small circle, make four inch-long cuts from the edge inward, as shown by the solid lines in figure 1. On the larger circle, cut out one quarter (figure 2). You will only need the other three quarters if you are going to make more than one mask. Turn the cut-out quarter into a cone and glue the seam (figure 3).

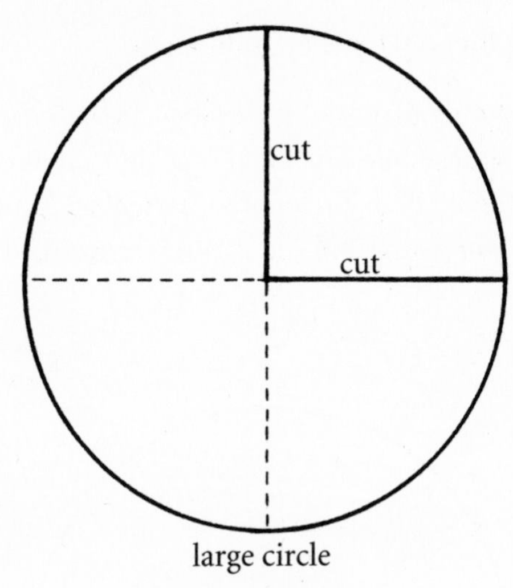

Lucka mask, figure 2

Lucka mask, figure 3

Using a large coin as a template, trace two eyeholes on the small circle as shown in figure 4. Cut out the eyeholes with your knife.

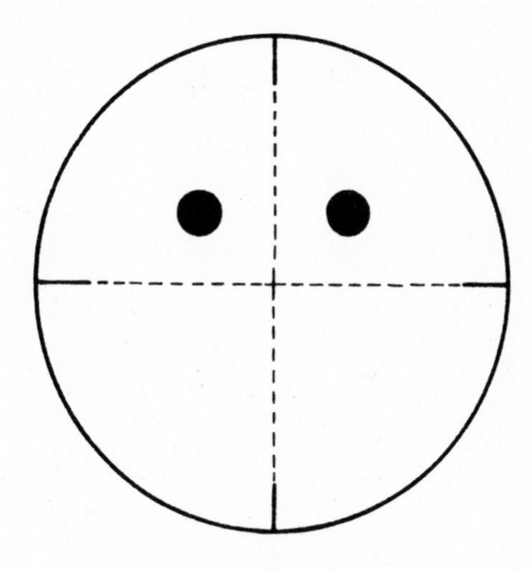

Lucka mask, figure 4

Use the base of your cone to trace a circle in the center of the mask. With your knife, divide the circle into "pie slices" as shown in figure 5, but *do not* cut out the circle itself. Fold the "pie slices" up and back as shown in figure 6.

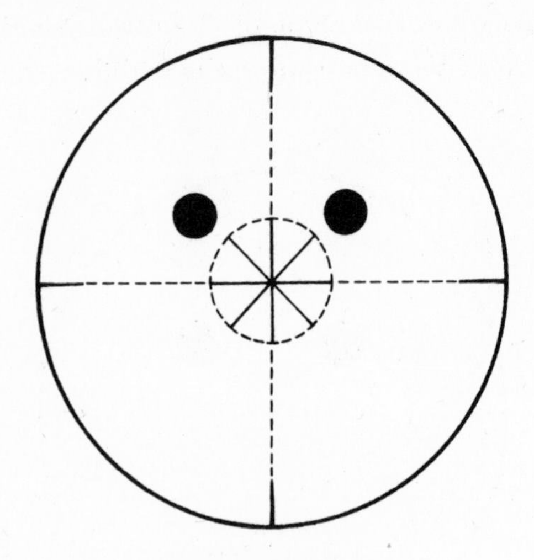

Lucka mask, figure 5

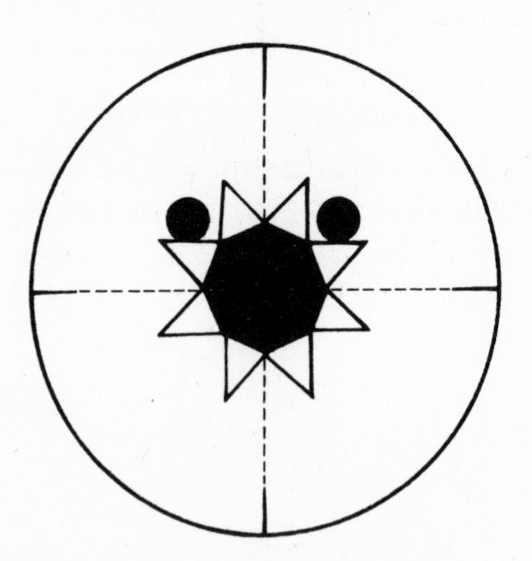

Lucka mask, figure 6

Slide the cone out through the hole in the center of the mask. Glue the "pie slices" to the base of the cone to hold it in place.

It's time to use those four cuts you made at the edge of the mask. Starting at the forehead, slide the edges of the cut one over the other and glue in place. Do the chin next, then the cheeks. Punch a hole at the side of each cheek and tie a length of yarn or ribbon in each hole.

Figure 7 shows the finished mask with silver glitter applied on the nose and around the eyeholes. There is no mouth because the Lucka traditionally does not speak.

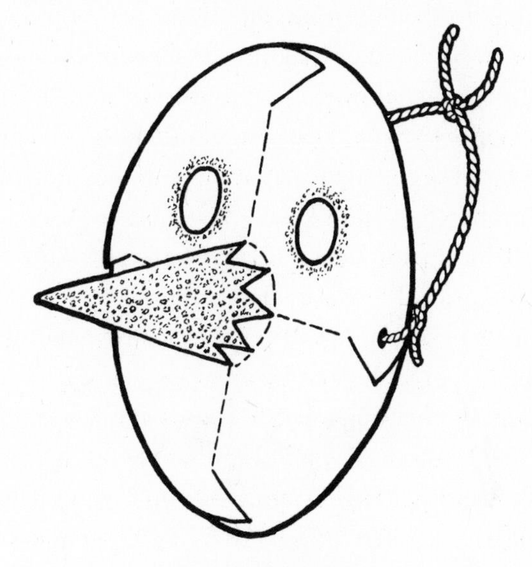

Lucka mask, figure 7

Rising from the Ashes

Meanwhile, in Bohemian Rosenberg, the *Lucu*, three youths dressed in white, entered the house with broom, bucket, and mop. Without a word, they proceeded to whisk and wash away until the housewife presented each of them with a small gift. Like the equally mysterious Slavic "Sweeper" who entered homes silently during Advent to brush the stove three times with her bundle of birch twigs, the Lucu's services were more of a blessing than a thorough cleaning.

Further to the east, there was a Slovakian Lucka who glided silently with face veiled through all the nights between her feast day and Christmas Eve. The Slovakian Lucka reminds us of both the Barborky and the scarecrow brides, who, not unlike those virginal Christian martyrs, were stabbed, burned, and/or cast into rivers.

Back in Sicily, Lucia Night is celebrated with bonfires, though the saint's image is never thrown into the flames. Lucia has proven herself to be one of the most resilient saints, having survived the Reformation in both the Lutheran and Anglican churches. There's really no need to feel sorry for her, especially when you take into account her striking resemblance to Aurora, Roman goddess of the dawn. If not Aurora, then the first Lucia was probably some native Sicilian equivalent thereof. In Sicily, she also served as a gift-giver, coming down the chimney in her witch's weeds, not her saintly garments. This Lucia threw ashes in the eyes of any child she caught spying on her. The saint, we are told, gouged her own eyes out to make herself less attractive to potential suitors, but the throwing of the ashes strikes one as a reminder never to look directly at the sun or at secretive gift-givers.

Regardless of whether or not she ever actually existed, the Sicilian Santa Lucia aspired to become the bride of Christ. Still a virgin, she now banishes the winter darkness with a brave display of candlelight. The Lucka and Lussibrud, on the other hand, consumed the night, taking it with her when she left the village so that the hours of daylight might increase. In

Bohemia, she was said to "drink the night." This older Lucy was the bride of Death, the midwinter darkness her dowry. As such, she provided an invaluable service to the far-flung communities of farmers and herdsmen to which she had been born. No Christian saint could quite replace her.

With the Old Solstice behind us and Christmas on its way, have we now seen the last of the glowing, bridelike Midwinter Witch? No, we have not, for, as the cast-down White Witch in *Prince Caspian* says herself, "[W]ho ever heard of a witch that really died? You can always get them back."

CHAPTER TEN

There Are Witches in the Air

It was once the custom of Austrian farm wives to go out to the orchard at midnight on St. Andrew's Eve (November 29) to break branches from the apricot trees. They forced the branches into flower in vases at home, then carried them to church on Christmas Eve. The white blossoms must have looked quite striking against the wives' dark wool Sunday dresses, but it was not these ladies' intention to create a pretty tableau; the flowering apricot branch allowed the bearer to pick out any witches in the congregation. What set the Austrian witch apart? Well, if you had an apricot branch, you would notice she carried a wooden pail on her head. I don't know about witches, but the practice must have been an effective means of identifying the parish busybodies.

St. Andrew's Day is an important fingerpost along the road to Christmas. There are two systems in place for calculating the beginning of Advent, the ecclesiastical Christmas season. One is to count back from the fourth Sunday before Christmas Day. The other is to locate the Sunday closest to St. Andrew's Day. In most Catholic and formerly Catholic regions, St. Andrew's Day is the cue to start planning a happy holiday, but it is the darker occasion of St. Andrew's Eve, and the ensuing Christmas season, which concerns us here.

Vampires

While the Austrian witches were scouring their milk pails and Polish girls were busy pouring lead into cold water to find out when and to whom they would be married, the Romanians had bigger problems. In Romania, St. Andrew's Eve was not a night to go out, let alone to go wandering in the orchard. It was not enough to lock the doors; before dark, all apertures had to be thoroughly rubbed with a peeled garlic clove, for on this night the vampires clawed their way out of their graves and walked again. Carrying their coffins portage-style, they paraded into the village to circle their former homes before taking themselves to the crossroads to engage in a pitched battle, no doubt with the vampires of the neighboring village.

A cross placed, chalked, or painted over a door or cattle stall imparts protection to the occupant, but a cross*roads* has always been the haunt of witches and other "malevolent" spirits, perhaps because suicides were buried and outlaws left to rot there. The Apostle Andrew, whose night this is, was martyred on an X-shaped cross. His feast day marks a crossroads within the year, for it was acknowledged in much of Europe as the true beginning of winter.

Joining these more usual vampires at the crossroads were the village's congenital vampires. This could be a seventh son or an individual whose mother had neglected to pull out the one or two teeth with which he had been born. The soul of this kind of vampire left his sleeping body as a blue flame flying out through the mouth. Between home and the crossroads, it assumed the shape of that vampire's personal animal, so even the nosy neighbor who was brave enough to peer out the window would have no idea to whom the fiery blue dog flying by might belong. Cockcrow sent both species of vampire scuttling back to their graves and their beds on the morning of St. Andrew's Day.

In his mammoth work *The Golden Bough*, Sir James George Frazer describes another sort of "vampyre" afoot in Romania. This one might be kept at bay with the "need fire," which was kindled afresh after all fires in the community had been extinguished. The need fire was used to purify and protect the cattle from diseases that these vampires were thought to cause. Unlike Bram Stoker's or Stephenie Meyer's undead, these vampyres were incorporeal.[37] Frazer contrasts them with "living witches," classing them instead with "other evil spirits." Though filtered first through German and then through French, the term *vampire* arrived in English almost untouched from Serbian. The word is so old that its etymology is uncertain, though it may have come from the Turkish *ubyr*, which means simply "witch."

Down with a Bound

Long before the introduction of "floo-powder," there was already a lot of coming and going through the fireplace flue as the witches floated very nimbly both up and down the chimbley. In Somerset, the general consensus was that witches could not walk through walls at Christmas or at

37. For a thorough treatment of some distressingly corporeal vampires, see Paul Barber's book *Vampires, Burial, and Death*, if you have the stomach for it.

any other time of the year; that was for ghosts. Most often, witches entered the house through the door or window just like everyone else. White or gray witches were able to walk in the church door to attend Midnight Mass, but black witches had to stay outside or risk becoming distinctly unwell. The Somerset witch's favorite route, however, was through the chimney, and in this she was not alone.

In Norway, too, Christmas Eve was a great traveling night for witches. Not just brooms but stools, staves, and fireplace tools were hidden away to prevent the witches from stealing and riding them. This, of course, was no obstacle to the witch who possessed an Icelandic witch's bridle, for she could transform anything, even a washboard, into a fast-moving vehicle just by laying the bridle upon it. Where there's a witch, there's a way, and many of them probably kept their own stashes of extra broomsticks under the floorboards or in secret cupboards under the stairs.[38] The typical folkloric witch also had a hornful of flying ointment with which she could anoint household objects to make them hover in the air like spaceships.

38. Such a stash was discovered in an old house in Wellington, England, in 1887, when demolition work revealed a hidden room inside the attic containing a comfy chair, a collection of six heather brooms, and a rope into which crow, rook, and white goose feathers had been woven. This "witch's ladder," as it was identified by the workmen, was apparently used to work black magic, not to get from one place to another. In his book *History of Wellington*, A. L. Humphreys suggests it was used to cross from rooftop to rooftop, but surely that was what the brooms were for? Taking their cue from early Wiccan writers such as Gerald Gardner, modern Witches use the witches' ladder, also known as a "wishing rope" or sewel, to work white magic. The last occupant of the house in Wellington was an old woman. How she was supposed to have gotten in and out of the hidden room where she kept her broomsticks we are not told.

Knowing all this, Norwegian peasants spent the darkest hours of Christmas Eve trying to shoot the witches out of the sky like pigeons. But if you wanted to save your buckshot, all you really had to do was call out the names of suspected witches, causing them to fall in mid-flight. Where were all of these witches supposed to be going? The bright meadows of Jönsås, a mountain in eastern Norway, were a popular destination at Easter and Midsummer, but on Christmas Eve, the place to be was "Blue Knolls." There, all the witches who had signed their names in the big book belonging to "Old Erik," as the Devil was fondly known, gathered in the snow to hold their own feast apart from the Christian folk on the farms below.

In his childhood memoir, *When I Was a Boy in Norway*, Dr. J. O. Hall claims that the English Yule log was originally a Norwegian import. If this is true, then the idea that the ashes of the Yule log will keep witches away probably also came from Norway. The Norwegian housewife who was still worried about witches sliding down the chimney on Christmas Eve could throw salt on the flames of the Yule log, for there was nothing like a blue fire to deter a witch.

While the presence of a glittering Christmas tree was not enough to keep a witch out, dried spruce boughs laid on the fire might, for the dry needles created an explosion of sparks that frightened the witches away. Today, firecrackers are used to the same end, but are they as effective? It may not have been just the flash and the noise that was supposed to put the witches off but the concentrated essence of evergreen. Throughout Europe, on all the most dangerous nights of the year, the farmer made the rounds of his outbuildings with a brush and a bucket of pine tar, for the vigorously turpentiney scent of pine tar, which many of us find pleasantly heady, is apparently repellent to witches.

Scandinavians have been distilling tar from the split roots of *Pinus sylvestris* since time out of mind. In the old days, the distillation process took place in earth-covered kilns in the forest, so perhaps Snorri Sturluson's dark elves were actually ancient kiln-watchers. The Norsemen used pine tar to waterproof their boats when they went a-viking, using the leftovers in the bucket to paint black crosses, or in those days Thor's hammers, above the farmhouse door and above each stall in the cow byre. Just about anywhere in Europe where pine trees grew, pine-tar crosses were painted at strategic points around the homestead. Such crosses could be stroked onto the beams at any time, but they should be given a fresh coat at Walpurgis Night, Midsummer, and, of course, Christmas Eve.

Rise of the House of Knusper

On December 23, 1893, Engelbert Humperdinck's *Hansel and Gretel*, a "fairy opera," premiered at the Hoftheater in Weimar with Richard Strauss conducting. This was the beginning of a Christmas tradition that has lasted to this day, but it was also the most recent development in an older, edible Germanic tradition. Eighty-one years earlier, the story of Hansel and Gretel first appeared in print in *Household Stories* by the Brothers Grimm. "Hansel and Gretel," the fairy tale, is an example of Tale Type 327, in which a child or children defeat an ogre or witch. Tale Type 327 is found all over Europe, so who knows how old it might be? One theory is that it grew out of the Great Famine of 1315–1320, but this theory overlooks the fact that poverty and hunger were ongoing issues for peasant families until very recent times.

Even before the opera's premiere, "Hansel and Gretel" was considered a Christmas story, perhaps because it featured an edible house.[39] The Brothers Grimm say only that the witch's house "was built of bread and roofed with cakes," but few Germans would consider building a witch's house out of anything but *Lebkuchen*. What is the difference between Lebkuchen and gingerbread? Lebkuchen, which is eaten in many shapes throughout the Christmas season, contains no ginger. The *Lebkuchenhäuschen*, which also goes by the names *Hexenhäuschen* ("witch's cottage") and *Knusperhäuschen* ("crunchy cottage"), and even "*Knisper-Knasper-Knusperhaus*," as it is referred to in Act I of the opera, is a staple of the German, Swiss, and Austrian Christmas. In the folk song "Hänsel und Gretel," of uncertain date, the witch's house is made of *Pfefferkuchen*, another ubiquitous German Christmas cookie that comes coated in hard white icing. So perhaps the snow-bedecked witch's house represents a Christmas tradition independent of either the Grimms or the Humperdincks.

It was the composer's sister, Adelheid Wette, who, working from the Grimms' story, wrote a poem about Hansel and Gretel for her children to perform at home on Christmas. No

39. "The Three Little Men in the Wood," another of the Grimms' fairy tales, was apparently never even in the running to become a seasonal opera, even though it opens in the snowbound forest. "The Three Little Men" features the almost universal "berries in winter" folktale motif as well as incorporating elements of Cinderella, Snow White, and Frau Holle, with the heroine taking on shades of White Lady toward the end of the tale. But, unlike "Hansel and Gretel," "The Three Little Men" has neither a witch nor a Lebkuchen house, so I suppose there was really no contest.

doubt this was one of those dreaded recitations that many German children are still forced to deliver in front of the decorated tree on Christmas Eve. In Adelheid's version, the mother sends the children out in a fit of temper; it's not premeditated abandonment. She is not nearly as heartless as the stepmother in the Grimms' version of the story, who sniffs, "Better get the coffins ready!" when the children's father balks at her plan. Just to confuse the issue, many productions cast the same singer as both the mother and the witch. At other times, the witch may be sung by a male tenor, while the role of Hansel is often sung by a woman.

The opera does not actually take place at Christmastime; the only fir trees are the ones clustered at the foot of the Ilsenstein where the witch's cottage appears. In the first act, the father, a broom-maker, mentions that the villagers are preparing for a feast. This is probably St. John's Day, or Midsummer, since his children are at the same time picking wild strawberries[40] at the foot of the aforementioned Ilsenstein, a knobbly stone protuberance poking its head out of the dark forest of the Harz in order to get a good look at the nearby Brocken, a mountain known by all Germans to be heavily frequented by witches. Coming home drunk, the father boasts to his wife that he has sold his entire stock of besoms. One cannot help but wonder if he might have sold one of them to the Nibbling Witch, who will soon try to cook his children, for the Nibbling Witch likes to circle her house on a broomstick.

40. In "The Three Little Men," the wicked stepmother sends the unnamed heroine out in a paper frock to gather strawberries in the snow.

If you don't already know how it all ends, or even if you do, you can host a showing of *Hansel and Gretel* at home. There are a number of productions from which to choose. You might try the 1998 DVD *Hänsel und Gretel* directed by Frank Corsaro, in which the sets and costumes are designed by Maurice Sendak. (I, for one, would not dare to take a bite out of Sendak's witch's house no matter how hungry I was; it has eyes!) Unfortunately, there is no DVD of Tim Burton's live-action, strongly Japanese-flavored *Hansel and Gretel,* which appeared on the Disney Channel on Halloween 1983. Like most of the world, I've never actually seen Burton's version, but it can't be any creepier than the 1954 stop-action *Hansel and Gretel: An Opera Fantasy* directed by Michael Myerberg. For movie snacks, I suggest almonds and raisins, the foods the witch fed to Hansel to fatten him up.

Craft/Recipe: Lebkuchen Witch's House

Before you decide that this project is too much for you, keep in mind that Lebkuchen is rolled out much thicker than gingerbread cookie dough. These thicker walls make the house quite easy to assemble.

The following instructions will make one Witch's House about 4 inches high, 4½ inches wide, and 6 inches long in a garden that's about 5½ inches wide and 8 inches long, with a little dough left over for details like shutters, paving stones, animal familiars, or whatever else you can dream up. Or, you can bake the extra dough into cookies for immediate eating. Because I like a hollow chimney through which smoke can escape, I build mine out of dark chocolate segments. My German grandmother, however, made hers out of a solid, heavy piece of dough. When the chimney fell in, it was time to eat the house.

Overhanging eaves are another hallmark of the traditional Witch's House. This leaves lots of room for icicles, which can be made with a quick sweep of a fork or knife. Since this is a humble, homemade sort of cottage, you will not be called upon to wrestle with a pastry bag.

In Germany, the door of the Witch's House is usually left ajar to entice Hansel and Gretel inside. An open door also allows you to put a tea light inside to illuminate the windows, which can be glazed with dried lemon or orange slices, Fruit Roll-Ups, or—my personal favorite—small sheets of roasted seaweed. If you make a hollow chimney, the smoke from the blown-out tea light will drift up through it.

The green seaweed windows combined with a lot of black licorice accents will convey a sense of poorly suppressed witchiness. I have placed two Trader Joe's Black Licorice Scottie Dogs in my garden along with a chocolate Christmas tree for their convenience. (You could also put a few black licorice cats on the roof.) For a final touch, I snipped the end of a black licorice stick into a brush and left it sticking out of the chimney. We can only hope that the chimney sweep to whom it belonged did not end up in the witch's oven!

Step 1: The Template

All you need to make a template is a sheet of 8½" x 11" paper, a pencil, and a pair of scissors. Draw the pieces as shown or enlarge on a photocopier. (You don't have to cut out the window in the side wall; you can use a water-bottle cap to cut it out of the dough later.) Cut out all your template pieces and set them aside before you make your dough.

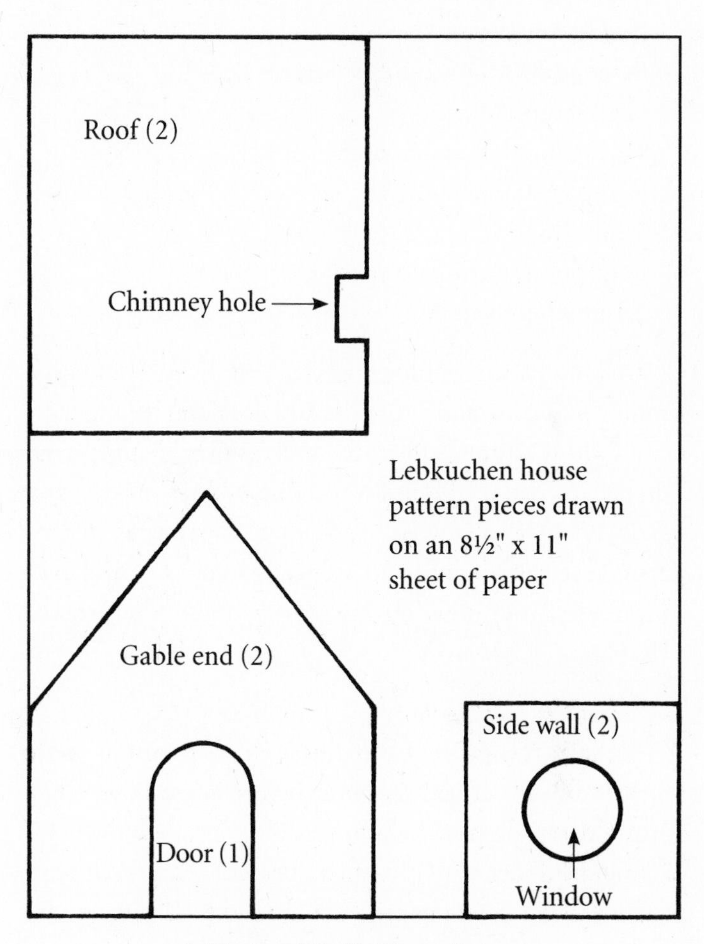

Lebkuchen Witch's House, figure 1

Step 2: The Dough

Ingredients:

5 Tablespoons unsalted butter, softened

1½ cups sugar

2 eggs, gently beaten
Zest of one lemon
½ teaspoon ground cloves
½ teaspoon nutmeg
1½ teaspoons cinnamon
½ cup ground almonds
3 cups flour
2 teaspoons baking powder
2 Tablespoons milk

Cream butter and sugar together in a large bowl. Stir in eggs, lemon zest, spices, and almonds. Add flour and baking powder a little at a time, adding the milk as the dough stiffens. You will have to work the last half-cup of flour in with your hands. When it's all mixed, shape it into a loaf, wrap in plastic, and refrigerate until you are ready to cut out and bake the pieces of your house. If you're ready right now, proceed to step 3.

Step 3: Cutting and Baking

If you have refrigerated the dough, leave it out at room temperature for at least an hour before beginning. When you are ready, preheat oven to 425°F.

Roll the dough out to ¼-inch thickness. Place your template pieces on the dough and cut around each with a sharp knife. Placing the template pieces as close to each other and as close to the edges of the dough as possible will minimize the number of times you need to roll out the dough. Remember: you need two gable ends, two roof pieces, and two side walls. You can add a window in the gable end without the door.

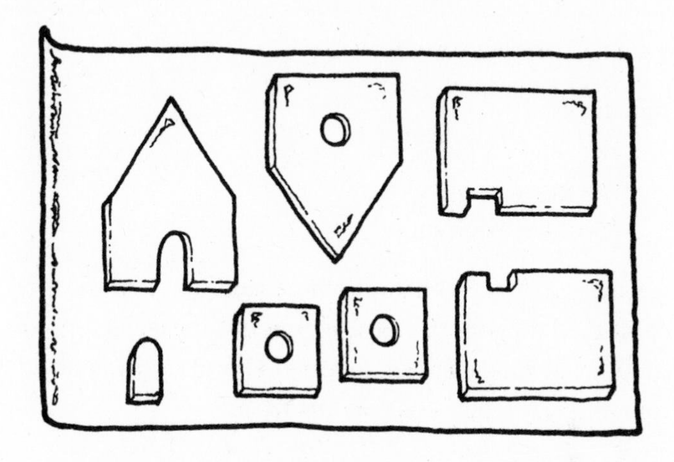

Lebkuchen house pieces laid out on a cookie sheet

Lebkuchen Witch's House

When all the house pieces are cut out, roll and cut out your garden.

Place all the pieces carefully on one or more cookie sheets lined with nonstick foil and bake for 15 minutes or until golden brown. If in doubt, it's better to over-bake them than to under-bake them. Here's one rule of thumb: when your kitchen starts to smell like the Old World Christmas, your Lebkuchen is almost done.

Let the pieces cool *completely* before you make the icing and assemble the house. You can even put the pieces in a tin and pick them up again the next day.

Step 4: The Icing

The icing is your snow as well as the glue that will hold your house together. This recipe makes more than enough, so don't be stingy with it. Also, don't worry if the finished house looks a little gloppy; that's how your friends will know you made it yourself.

Ingredients:

- 2 egg whites
- ¼ teaspoon cream of tartar
- 2 cups powdered sugar

Beat the egg whites with the cream of tartar until the mixture foams. Add the sugar a little at a time, beating on low speed. Continue beating a few more minutes until the icing hangs from the beaters but does not drip off.

Step 5: Assembly and Decoration

First, spread the yard with a thick layer of icing. Press one gable wall and adjacent side wall into the icing, cementing the corner with more icing. Check that they are standing straight, then add the remaining two walls and the open door. Let the icing dry about 20 minutes before gluing the roof on. Cover the bowl of icing with plastic wrap to prevent any crust from forming. While you are waiting for the walls to dry, glue your choice of fruit or seaweed inside the windows.

Lebkuchen Witch's House

After you have cemented the roof pieces in place, you can assemble the chimney. Cut the chocolate pieces at a slant to match the slope of the roof. You don't have to be too precise; a healthy slather of icing will cover any mistakes.

Use the rest of the icing for icicles and to glue on any decorations. The possibilities are endless. I am partial to the aforementioned licorice pets and sticks as well as licorice allsorts and starlight mints.

Step 6: Eating

Though you might need a hammer, there's no reason why you can't eat this house when Christmas is over. In fact, it's a good excuse for a party. Hold each shard of house over a steaming cup of coffee or tea to soften it. The seaweed window panes can be easily peeled off, since Lebkuchen and seaweed together is not a taste that can be acquired by all.

Witches Bearing Gifts

There was a time when it was considered godly to walk around in a flea-infested hair shirt, while cleanliness was next to witchiness. To this day, the Italian witch Befana pays the price for her overzealous housekeeping each Epiphany Eve when she flies over the rooftops on her broomstick, searching for the Baby Jesus. Like the other Midwinter Witches who have been renamed for saints, Befana's name is a slurring of her feast day, *Epiphania,* which comes from the Greek for "manifestation." Though Befana is now a thoroughly Christian witch, she remains a manifestation not just of that shining star over Bethlehem, but also of the old winter goddess who used to be abroad at Yuletide.

Befana had the chance to meet the Holy Family in person way back in the first century when the Three Kings stopped to ask for directions, but she was too busy sweeping the dust from her dooryard to pay the glittering company any mind. Of course, as soon as they rounded the bend, she had a change of heart and decided she really would like to bring a gift to this bright young baby. By the time she had changed her clothes and baked a batch of *pefanino,* or Epiphany biscuits, the caravan had passed out of sight. So began her two-thousand-year quest to locate and present her gifts to the Baby Jesus.

In Italy and the Italian-speaking regions of Switzerland, it is Befana who delivers the presents on the night of January 5. In Sicily, she goes by *La Vecchia di Natale*, the Old Christmas Woman, and comes on Christmas Eve—if, that is, she has not been preceded down the chimney by a sooty Lucia on the night of December 12. Usually, Befana simply pours the toys down the chimney, into the polished boots and striped stockings the children put out before they go to bed. How does Befana know what they want? Magic: the children write their lists on slips of paper in front of the fireplace and let them waft up the chimney and into the sky, where Befana deftly catches them.

Sometimes, the old hag comes inside to get a good look at the children themselves. One of these nights, she hopes, she'll finally meet up with the Christ Child. In the meantime, she's not above taking the naughty ones and eating them, though this aspect of her character has been played down in recent years. In the nineteenth century, the children of the house used to dress a rag doll as a witch and set it in the window on Befana's Eve. Today, you can still buy carved or stuffed Befanas at the Christmas markets in Italy.

Recipe: Befana Stars

The pefanino of earlier days was either round or shaped like Befana herself on her broomstick. If you are lucky enough to own a witch-shaped cookie cutter, go for it. Otherwise, the more contemporary star shape will do. Yes, I do realize that you're busy cleaning house after a frantic Christmas season, but take a hint from Befana, put down the broom, and bake some cookies.

For the dough:

- 1 stick (8 Tablespoons) unsalted butter, softened
- ¾ cup sugar
- 1 whole egg plus one egg yolk (reserve white for topping)
- Zest of one clementine or small orange
- Zest of one small lemon (use half for the dough, reserve other half for topping)
- ½ teaspoon vanilla extract
- ½ teaspoon anise extract
- 2 cups flour
- ½ teaspoon baking powder

Cream the butter and sugar together, add egg yolk, and stir well. Mix in zests and extracts. Add the baking powder to the flour and mix with the rest of the ingredients a little at a time. When the dough is smooth, form it into a ball, wrap it in plastic wrap, and refrigerate it for at least one hour.

For the topping:

- 1 egg white
- ¼ cup sugar
- Remaining lemon zest
- ½ cup ground almonds (or you can use sliced almonds and chop them very fine)
- Powdered sugar

In a deep, medium-sized bowl, beat the egg white and sugar until stiff. Fold in lemon zest and almonds. Set aside.

Roll out the dough to ⅛-inch thickness on a floured surface and cut into star shapes. Lay stars on a greased or parchment-lined cookie sheet and drop a dollop of topping in the center of each star. Bake at 350°F for 13 minutes or until star points and topping are golden brown.

Dust cookies with powdered sugar while they are still warm.

Befana stars

CHAPTER ELEVEN

Dark Spirits of Hearth and Home

The Lithuanian girl who wished to look on the face of her future husband could do so by walking three times round the chimneystack, naked, on Christmas Eve. This would be the central, freestanding structure that rose right up through the attic, so the girl could enact the ritual in private. The attic was really the only place to do it, for there could be no lights burning in the room if the spell were to work and her lover's image come swimming up out of the darkness. It is not by chance that the magic was worked in the vicinity of the chimney, for the space inside those creosote-caked bricks or stones housed powerful spirits, as did the hearth below.

First engineered by the Normans in the eleventh century, the chimney was much more than a means of conducting smoke out of the hall. If you wish to look with your own eyes on the passage to the land of the dead, you have only to find an ancient Welsh farmhouse, step inside, and stick your head inside the kitchen fireplace. Twist your head and look up into the black flue. Can you see a light at the end of the tunnel? For many a Welshman who had died or been laid out at home, this was the way to the afterlife. It was bad practice to carry a corpse out the same door used by the living, and the windows were too small to accommodate a coffin. There was, however, plenty of room to hoist one up and out the massive brick chimney. Elsewhere in the world, and no doubt within Wales itself, house builders hit upon the more convenient solution of a "coffin door," which could be opened up easily when needed but blended in with the wood paneling when not. Still, in remote parts of Wales, the chimney remained the way to go.

It's possible that the practice of extracting the dead through the chimney was once more widespread, as in those distant days when, as Gerald Gardner would have it, the houses were built into the hillsides, and the living, too, might go to and fro through the smoke hole. And if the dead could escape *up* the chimney, might not a few wayward spirits come tumbling down? While the witch used the chimney mostly to depart and re-enter her own home, the Bodach, a Scottish version of the black-faced English bogeyman, liked to frequent other people's chimneys. If he heard there were some particularly bad children up in the nursery, he might avail himself of the flues to get at them. There are few descriptions of the Bodach, since most of his victims were successfully scrobbled up the chimney and never heard from again, but he was supposed to resemble a little old man.

In addition to the ghosts and bogeys sidling along the sooty passageways, there were ancestral spirits who slept all year among the hearth stones, then flared up brilliantly at

Christmas to dispense their gifts and glowing blessings on the home. You will recall the story of the Gilbertsons' boggart, who packed himself in the butter churn so he wouldn't be left behind when the family decided to "flit." Had the story taken place a thousand or more years earlier, the Gilbertsons would not have thought of moving at all; they would have recognized the so-called boggart as a member of the family, perhaps even its most powerful member.

The Gilbertson boggart, like most boggarts these days, no longer had a proper name. Under pressure from a changing world, the family had long ago forgotten it. Throughout Europe, the names of the ancestors have faded away along with their cults,[41] but there was one part of the house in which these tutelary ghosts lingered into the late nineteenth century and to which they still return at Yule. It is the hearth, the glowing throne of the household gods.

On Christmas Eve we hang our stockings in front of the fireplace not because we don't have clothes dryers or because St. Nicholas can't fill them any other way—he's a worker of wonders, after all—but because the fireplace remains a sacred space, a sooty temple, if you will. Even when the hearth amounts to nothing more than a closed range, it is still the heart of the home. A very, very long time

41. They did not disappear all at once; in Lithuania, where such rituals went on a lot longer than elsewhere on the continent, the hearth spirit Gabija was addressed respectfully each morning when the fire was stoked and again at bedtime when the embers were banked. When a bride departed for her new home, she carried with her the fire from her mother's hearth. In Ireland, St. Brigid (formerly the goddess Brigid) was invoked each evening when the central hearth fire was covered over with ashes.

ago, the remains of the ancestors themselves were interred underneath the stones surrounding the open hearth, their long bones forced into fetal position and dusted with red ochre. Even into the Christian era, infants who expired before baptism might be buried under the doorstep, beneath the easily loosened cobbles in front of the fireplace, or bricked up in a new chimney to serve as the home's guardian forever after.

The Kallikantzaros

As evinced by the Scottish Bodach, not all chimney sprites were kind. Even the Bodach, who was a year-round menace, could not hold a candle to that most horrible of Christmas chimney-climbers, the southern Greek *kallikantzaros* or *karkantzaros.* The kallikantzaros was red-eyed and covered in black hair, its overlong tongue marking it as Čert's and Krampus's close kin. Instead of goat's hooves, however, it had club-feet or just one foot. This did not stop it from getting where it wanted to go. Traveling in packs, these creatures snuck in by way of the chimney to devour Christmas dinner. Not only did they gobble up the Christmas sweets and all the roast pork, of which they were especially fond, but they also felt a need to trash the place before clambering back up the chimney.

Those with Christmas birthdays were most likely to be transformed into kallikantzaroi. They have been tentatively identified as Turkish werewolves marauding over the border, but the kallikantzaros also resembles an ancient Greek bogeyman with a soot-blackened face whose mission it was to snatch misbehaving children. Like the Romanian vampires, some of whom assumed their troubling shapes only on certain days of the year, many kallikantzaroi were ordinary mortals most of the time. Others were year-round monsters, though they showed themselves only at Christmas.

The kallikantzaros' taste for sweets suggests that it may be a vengeful child ghost like the Faroese niðagrisur, or "pig from below," while its appetite for pork might be the mark of a child-devourer. On the maternal side, the kallikantzaros is probably descended from a class of child-eating demons called *lamiae*. The lamiae were black-skinned and often depicted with a bird's or animal's feet, sometimes one of each or even three. Lamia was a mortal woman who was driven mad with grief when her own children were murdered by the goddess Hera. The lamiae continued to feast on unbaptized babies into the early modern era. Pork in the form of a pink-skinned suckling pig may originally have been offered to the kallikantzaroi in place of a newborn baby.

If you did not want the kallikantzaroi entering your house—and who would?—you could try hanging gifts of food, including pork chops, sausages, and candies, inside the chimney to pay them off. This had to be done not just on Christmas Eve but throughout the Twelve Days of Christmas. You could also try painting a black cross on the door. But the only surefire way of eradicating these demons was the application of frankincense and holy water. When the village priest arrived at the Orthodox Epiphany to bless the home with his smoking censer and basil-sprig aspergillum, the kallikantzaroi were finished. They beat a hasty retreat to their own dark haunts somewhere underground, not to return until next Christmas Eve.

The Yule Log

At Christmastime especially, the ancient ones are present within the confines of the hearth. Their cult survives in bits and pieces in the traditions associated with the Yule log, clog, or block. From the Balkans, to Germany, France, and England, libations were poured over the log, not just to set it merrily on fire, but to give the household gods and goddesses something good to drink and to invite them out to join the rest of the family at the feast.

As important as the Yule log itself were the charred splinters, embers, and ashes left over at the close of the Twelve Days of Christmas, for these were the bits the ancestors had touched and transformed into magical gifts. Swept up as carefully as if they were gold, they were dispensed as needed throughout the year. In Germany, the fine ash of the *Christbrand* or *Christklotz* was strewn over the dormant fields on the nights between Christmas and Epiphany, while a charred hunk wedged in the crotch of a fruit tree ensured a good harvest. When tucked in the bed strings, it would protect the house from lightning, and when dropped down a well, it kept the water potable.

An elderly friend of mine can recall Christmas Eves in Charente-Inférieure (now Charente-Maritime) in western France when her grandfather dropped handfuls of popping corn in the ashes before the massive, glowing tree trunk in the fireplace. There, the kernels were transformed into what he called *dames blanches*, "white ladies," dancing in the heat of the fire. In Burgundy, they went one better, for there the smoldering log actually "gave birth" to little packets of sugar plums when the children weren't looking.

In most lands, the Yule log was not quite so fertile. Still, it was a treasure in itself, and on no account should any ashes be thrown away over the Christmas season. Ostensibly, this was so that one would not accidentally hit the Christ Child in the face, but originally, these ashes represented the family's fortunes and had therefore to be kept close. This explains why to part with even a spark of the home fire at this sacred time of year was to court disaster. Suppose the ancestors were offended at the casual lending out of their essence and decided to drift out the door after it?

Christmas is the season of good will, but if you were careless enough to let your own fire go out, you could not expect your neighbors to give you a light. The fizzling of the Yule flames was portentous on several levels. Before the tinderbox came along, it meant a cold bed and a cold board unless you could find some pre-Christmas embers still smoldering inside the village ash dump. It also meant there would be a death in the household within a year. Lastly and worst of all, it meant that the familial spirits had withdrawn their blessings and the very survival of the line was now in jeopardy. Even today, many families light a fat candle on Christmas Eve, placing it in the sink instead of blowing it out when they leave for Midnight Mass.[42]

No matter if you have washed it with wine, cider, or grain alcohol, there was only one way to light a Yule log,

42. In 1966, WPIX in New York City came up with a no-maintenance solution to the age-old problem: a televised Yule log. It burned merrily all Christmas Eve to a soundtrack of popular Christmas carols, and if you watched it long enough and carefully enough, you would notice the log grow smaller, then larger, then smaller again every few minutes.

and that was with a bit of the previous year's log. The idea was that the Yule fire never really went out, and that no one, whether unbaptized baby or ancient granny, ever really died, for how could there be death where there was light, love, and warmth?

The First-Footer

When and if the revelers finally went to bed on each of the nights between Christmas and New Year's Eve, the Yule fire was carefully banked, then stirred to life again the next morning. The question of who was to wake the fire on the first morning of the new year was one requiring careful consideration. Oddly enough, he was not supposed to be a member of the household.

In the British Isles, he was known as the *first-footer*, and it was best to engage him in advance, for the wrong sort of person would bring the wrong sort of luck. Throughout Europe, there was an all-but-universal consensus that the first-footer should not be a woman or, especially in Scotland, a redhead. If the first person to step over your threshold on New Year's Day is Nicole Kidman, then you might as well pack your bags and start over somewhere else, and if she happens to enter with her left foot, then there's really no help for you at all.

One of the oldest obligations of the first-footer—who was preferably tall, dark, handsome, and had been born feet first—was to stir the embers of the fire. He would do this before even greeting the master of the house, having first entered without knocking. The Macedonian first-footer paid homage to the resident spirits by first offering a stone or green twig at the altar of the hearth. Elsewhere in the Balkans, the *polaznik*, or "attendant," arrived first thing on Christmas Day to strike sparks from the Yule log. The more sparks the better, for each represented a sheep, chicken, or moment of happiness in the coming year.

The Chimneysweep

In England, the most desirable first-footer of all was the climbing boy, as underage chimneysweeps were known in the days when there was no such thing as underage, especially when it came to dangerous menial labor. When was the last time you had your chimney cleaned? In coal fire days, twice a year was the bare minimum; once in three months was more like it. Skip the chimneysweep, and you would eventually be woken up one night by a noise like trickling sand followed by a soft crash as, in the moonlight, a black creature materialized in the fireplace. Larger and larger it grew, climbing slowly, silently into the room. Could it be one of the dreaded Whisht Hounds that haunt the moors at Christmastime? No; it was a clod of accumulated creosote that had dislodged itself from the chimney's brick lining and fallen on the grate to rise up in a black cloud, besmirching furniture, carpets, and curtains.

Those of us who burn only candles and the occasional birch log in the fireplace would be unprepared for the amount of soot produced by a coal fire. By the early 1800s, coal had replaced wood as the preferred kitchen fuel and, except in peat-burning areas, it remained the fuel of choice for a long time afterward. The transition from wood to coal led to the shrinking of the fireplace, which led in turn to the widespread replacement of the Yule log with the Yule candle. The popularity of coal also transformed the chimneysweep from a mere tradesman to a talisman. Because coal burns so much more messily than wood, do-it-yourself chimney cleaning became less of an option. Even the poorest families had to engage a professional chimneysweep now and then.

The chimneysweep is a popular subject of the glassblowers of Lausitz in eastern Germany, who, for the last hundred years, have been furnishing the world with feather-light glass Christmas ornaments. Clasping his ladder and brushes close to his body, my own stout little chimneysweep in his black top hat looks a lot like a snowman, but such are the limits of the medium of blown glass. As German lucky symbols go, the chimneysweep is right up there with the horseshoe, the *Glückspilz*, and the marzipan pig. To this day, the sight of a well-dressed chimneysweep with a sprig of holly stuck in his hatband will bring a smile to anyone's face, especially in Germany and Denmark. The ladder and brushes he carried were the tools of his trade, but the top hat was the sweep's own talisman: it was supposed to prevent him from tumbling off the roof while he plied his brushes from above.

The washerwoman and the undertaker, whose cast-offs the sweeps had adopted for their uniforms, were just as indispensable to nineteenth-century urban life, but you don't see either of *them* adorning people's Christmas trees, nor would you invite them to step over your threshold on New Year's Day. There is something simply magical about a well-dressed chimneysweep, even, or especially, when he is coated in soot.

Since the Middle Ages, those Danish and German sweeps had been organized into guilds. The Jutish chimneysweep, who, as a rule, was a grown man and not a scrawny child, cut a dashing figure as he cycled through the streets, brushes strapped to his back, coat tails flying behind him. There were no gold buttons or frock coats for the English climbing boys, but by the mid-1800s, they had come to be regarded as such auspicious figures that you could assure yourself a whole year's good luck just by having one come and stand in your kitchen on New Year's Day. That was the one day of the year[43] when, instead of risking his life among London's narrow, carbon-coated flues, he could wander the neighborhoods with his fellows, accepting treats in exchange for the blessings he bestowed.

Obviously, the chimneysweep's nineteenth- and early-twentieth-century patrons did not consciously regard him as an intermediary between the household spirits and the living members of the family. By that time, a fireplace was just a fireplace and no longer a temple. But people did continue to look upon the chimneysweep as something more than what met the eye. Was it his blackened countenance

43. The English climbing boy did have one other day off and that was May Day, when he was allowed to lay his brushes aside and was given plenty to eat. American climbing boys enjoyed no such day and, unlike their English counterparts who were practically slaves, the American chimneysweeps often actually were slaves. Even in northern cities like New York, small boys were rented out from Southern slave owners and brought north to do the job. The use of underage chimneysweeps went on a lot longer in the United States than in England, where the practice effectively came to an end in 1875.

that placed him among the other dark yet indispensable Christmas spirits?

The age of coal should have fostered a dramatic rise in chimney revenants or unquiet ghosts, for, all too often, the climbing boy became wedged inside the flue and choked to death on the fine soot his movements dislodged. Then the bricklayer, who was *not* a lucky talisman, had to be called to come and dislodge the corpse. The reason why the ghostly climbing boy seems never to have made it into oral tradition is probably because these children, most of whom were sold into their so-called apprenticeships, had no one to answer for them. Few homeowners would want it known that a child had died in their walls. In fact, the master of a wealthy house might not even know of it until he was presented with the bill for the dismantling and restoration of the brickwork. The master sweep would soon replace the dead boy with another orphan or penniless waif, and all would be forgotten. Since many climbing boys eventually succumbed to asthma, tuberculosis, and cancer of the scrotum, brought on by prolonged exposure to soot, there was no one left to tell the tale.

Way back in the wood-burning days of the late sixteenth century, we find every Englishman's favorite hobgoblin, Robin Goodfellow, forsaking his usual sylvan haunts to roam the streets of London disguised as a chimneysweep. "Ho! Ho! Hoh!" he cries as he runs amuck with his brushes in *The Mad Pranks and Merry Jests of Robin Goodfellow*. Despite the grim reality of his situation, it seems the stage was already set for the climbing boy to take on a little of the power of Faerie.

The Fairy Queen's Men

The chimneysweep's soot-streaked face was the natural consequence of his profession, but what of those roving characters who deliberately blackened their faces? The bellsnickle and other wild "Nicholases" liked to blacken their faces, as do Knecht Ruprecht and the Moorish Zwarte Piet to this day. We have not yet mentioned the most famous of the Three Kings, Balthasar, who is traditionally portrayed with the dark complexion of a sub-Saharan African, no matter that the Magi were Persians. But, with the exception of Zwarte Piet who is made to wriggle up and down the chimney in the bishop's stead, none of these characters have much to do with the chimney or the hearth. Or do they?

The so-called Screaming Skull of Bettiscombe Manor in Dorset may provide a missing link of sorts. This family heirloom, which had at all times to be kept in the vicinity of the house's main chimney, was supposed for a long time to have belonged to a West Indian man, a servant of one of the house's early masters. As long as it was left in place, the skull would protect the house from harm. It was later proven to have been a woman's, so who knows who its original owner was or how it came to be resting in the chimney nook. The important thing is that the tutelary spirit attached to the skull was believed to have been dark of face.

The association between the spirits immanent in the chimney at Christmastime (or throughout the year as at Bettiscombe Manor) and the appearance of dark skin, whether genuine or artful, has been going on for longer than anyone can remember. The current house at Bettiscombe Manor was built in 1694, but the pan-European first-footer, who was preferably both dark-haired and dark-complexioned, recedes into the mists of the pre-Christian past.

Could anyone blame us if we were to go looking among the morris dancers (read "Moorish" dancers) for clues to this mysterious association? The folklorists of the early 1900s found in England's morris dancers a tantalizing pantheon of prehistoric fertility gods. The so-called "Welsh Border Morris" appears to provide exactly what we are looking for: black-faced dancers wielding sticks in an early winter ritual as old as the land itself. But further probing reveals that the morris dance began as a courtly Christmas entertainment and can only be traced back as far as 1458.

So who *are* these strange characters supposed to represent? Dark elves? The ancient dead, grown black from lying so long in the cold ground? It is tempting to surmise that the office of the first-footer was originally executed by a priest who blackened his face and hair in order to impersonate either one of the ancestors or some long-forgotten deity of winter. More romantic still is the notion that he may have belonged to an aboriginal European people, this time raven-haired instead of red, that fled to the hills at the rippling advance of the Indo-Europeans. In this scenario, an uneasy truce is reached in which the votaries of the native fertility goddess are invited down at the winter solstice to bestow the blessings of the old goddess upon the new stewards of the land.

Of course, there may be a more prosaic explanation for the dark-faced Christmas spirit. We have already witnessed the use of masks to disguise and transform. Ever since the Roman Saturnalia went head to head with Christmas, the

Church had been speaking out against the wearing of masks. To dress as a devil was devilish in itself, except, of course, if you were trying to frighten the children into learning their catechism. Now and again throughout the Middle Ages and Early Modern period, the carving and wearing of *Larven* and the like were outlawed, for even though they had found legitimate employment with a saint, Čert, Krampus, and the Buttnmandln could still get out of hand. At such times, those who could not or would not resist the social and spiritual forces that compelled them to take on otherworldly personae could get around the law by simply blacking their faces.

Thus, a soot-blackened face came to signal both an alliance with the ancestral spirits, elves, and fairies and to mark the disguised person as something of a rebel. In June of 1451, a party of one hundred men went hunting in the Duke of Buckingham's forest. They helped themselves to over a hundred deer, but they were not professional poachers; they were ordinary men dissatisfied with their living conditions. Dressed in makeshift war gear, their faces obscured by fake beards and a thin coating of charcoal, they identified themselves as the servants not of King Henry nor, certainly, of the Duke of Buckingham, but of the "queen of the fairies."

Why black? Why not woad or red ochre as in the old days? For one thing, soot was more readily available—all you had to do was reach into the fireplace—and it obscured the features more effectively than flour. There was also a belief, handed down from antiquity, that black made the wearer invisible to the spirits of the dead. (That is why black is the color of mourning in the Western world: originally it was a means of protection, not an expression of sorrow.) We may never have a completely satisfying explanation for the dark-faced Christmas spirit, but it seems that, by blackening his face, the mummer, Bellsnickle, Knecht Ruprecht, or servant of the Fairy Queen could put one foot in the unknown and keep the other safely planted in the here and now.

CHAPTER TWELVE

A Christmas Witch's Herbal

Generally, the medieval herbal, or "herball," was much plainer than the medieval bestiary. The hand-drawn or woodblock illustration of each plant had to resemble the real thing if the book was to be of any use, while the entries had to convey the unique properties of each species and how it might be employed in the stillroom, kitchen, or hall. That is not to say that there was no room at all for fancy or folkloric musings. On the contrary, many flowers, trees, and roots were valued as much for their power to banish ghosts, reveal hidden treasures, and keep witches away as they were for their ability to relieve cough or indigestion.

The plant world's link to the supernatural has certainly been weakened in recent centuries, but it has not been broken. To this day, it is hard to talk about garlic without mentioning vampires, or to speak of mistletoe without bringing up the Druids in the same breath. This chapter is the sort of herbal that I imagine a well-traveled Frau Holle (whose name may actually be related to the root word for "holly") might put together, then leave open on the bench beside her for a little light Christmas reading while she sits spinning by the hearth.

There are no instructions here for making tinctures or brewing herbal teas. Both the apple and the lingonberry are edible, of course, as are the berries of the juniper and the hips and petals of the white rose. All the rest are highly poisonous and, like the others, are presented here for the sake of their relationship to Christmas and for the strange tales attached to them.

Mistletoe
(Viscum album)

Why do brides make such wonderful ghosts? Is it because they already have the right clothes on? This might hold true for those who met their doom during or since the Victorian era, when the white wedding dress came into fashion, but before that, European brides were as likely to wear red, silver, or even black. It is the bride's precarious position in life—one foot over the threshold of conjugal bliss, the other still planted in childhood—that puts her at risk. If the earth should break open between her slippered feet, she will teeter and tumble into the Otherworld, never to return except as a ghost. Set her wedding during the supernaturally unstable Christmas season, and the opportunity for thrills and chills increases. Of course, most weddings go off with scarcely a hitch. In the case of the Mistletoe Bride, the tragedy struck during the reception.

The occasion is a Christmas wedding, the scene the great hall of a castle or manor house hung with holly and bunches of mistletoe to celebrate the nuptials of Lord Lovel (or a nobleman of some other name) and his lady love, a playful slip of a girl. As the evening wears on, the bride suggests a game of hide-and-seek. But after her turn comes to hide, she cannot be found—not that night, nor the morning after, nor in the days and months that follow. She seems to have evaporated, leaving her new husband to pine away, but first he orders his lost bride's possessions stowed away in the attic so they will not remind him of his grief.

Years or decades after the bride's unfathomable disappearance, another family or branch of the family take possession of the place. They are sorting through the dusty old sticks of furniture when they happen upon an old chest, inside of which they find a skeleton in a wedding gown and crumbling bridal wreath. We are to understand that the girl either banged her head with the lid or got locked inside and suffocated during the infamous game of hide-and-seek.

The Mistletoe Bride was made famous by Thomas Haynes Bayly, whose wildly popular ballad "The Mistletoe Bough" was published around 1830. But did Bayly make the whole thing up? Not according to the owners and caretakers of a number of old houses scattered from Yorkshire to Cornwall, a few of them no more than collections of chimney stumps and empty arches rising up from well-tended lawns. At Brockdish Hall in Norfolk, there is supposed to be a Jacobean bust of the bride, while Minster Lovell in Oxfordshire has both the right family name and the story of a skeleton discovered in a secret space behind the chimney in 1708. But there were also Lovels at Skelton in Yorkshire. Both Bramshill House and Marwell Old Hall in Hampshire have since mislaid the famous chest, though Bramshill has managed to hold on to a ghostly "bride," who appears now and then in one of the bedrooms.

Samuel Rogers, writing about a decade before the publication of "The Mistletoe Bough," would make the heroine a juniper bride, for "Ginevra," the name he assigns to both the bride and his poem, means "juniper." By his own admission, it was Rogers' personal stroke of creativity to set the familiar tale in Modena, Italy. As a piece of folklore, the Mistletoe Bride is unique to the English-speaking world; there is no corresponding *Mistelbraut* motif in Germany, Bohemia, or anywhere else on the continent.

Even Lucy, smallest of the Pevensie children in *The Lion, the Witch and the Wardrobe*, knows you should never shut yourself in a wardrobe. The same goes for old dowry chests, although, since they can only be locked from the outside, it would be very tricky indeed to get stuck inside one. Silly as she might have been, the Mistletoe Bride has nevertheless earned her place among the unquiet Christmas spirits of the British Isles.

Mistletoe had long been accepted as a decoration in home and hall, but the idea that the mistletoe was not permitted among the Christmas greens in English churches is a common slander. The reason usually given is that mistletoe was sacred to the pagan Druids, but it could just as easily be a distant Germanic memory of the beloved god Balder's death by mistletoe, or the fact that twiggy growths of mistletoe on the trunks of trees were known as "witches' brooms." The early church fathers disapproved of any adorning of the pews and aisles with Christmas greens because it smacked of the pagan Kalends and Saturnalia. Still, English church wardens continued to haul such greens inside by the bushel, mistletoe included, even under Oliver Cromwell's rule, when the celebration of Christmas itself was illegal.

Not that the mistletoe really needed the church's approval; it already had an established place in the home, where bushy balls of mistletoe hung from the ceiling at Yuletide. Some of these balls were decorated like Christmas trees, with corn dollies, fruits, paper roses, ribbons, and candles. At first it was just to look at; widespread kissing under the mistletoe did not start until the 1700s, and for a long time it went on only below stairs. The mistletoe has been used to solicit kisses since time immemorial, but it used to involve chasing the girl down with sprig in hand, and then you could only kiss her as many times as there were berries. If it had been a bad year for mistletoe, the wooden hoops of the "kissing ball" could be covered in ivy or even the prickly gorse (*Ulex europaeus*), which could be gathered on the moor and might still have a few yellow flowers on it at Christmastime. Still, a token sprig of mistletoe, however scrawny, must hang from the bottom of the ball.

In the mountain inns of the Rhaetian Alps, on the Austrian side of the Swiss border, there used to lurk a sort of living kissing ball, though he was not at all pretty to look at. On the night of December 31, St. Sylvester's Day,[44] each inn installed its own *Silvester* in a dark corner of the tap room.

44. December 31 is St. Sylvester's feast day, but in German-speaking countries it is known as *Silvesterabend*, "Sylvester's Eve," while New Year's Day is simply *Silvester*. It seems that the identity of this fourth-century Roman pope was quickly subsumed by the festivities of the outgoing year when another pope, Innocent XII, fixed New Year's Day as January 1.

This Silvester did not represent the fourth-century pope for which he was named any more than the Pelznichol could be said to portray the Bishop of Myra; he was the incarnation of the old year, or its last gasp, and he was eager for a kiss before he went on his way. Wearing the mask of an old man with a long white beard and a mistletoe wreath on his head, he must have looked like a withered Father Christmas as he sat there in the gloom beyond the hearth light. There he waited for someone—anyone—to forget himself or herself and cross beneath the wreath of pine boughs hanging from the ceiling. As soon as the hapless drinker did so, Silvester leapt up and planted a rough kiss on his or her lips. When the clock struck twelve, the fun was over, for at that moment Silvester was driven out into the snow.

The Rhaetians, who gave their name to this stretch of the Alps, were an ancient Alpine people who may have been Etruscan, Celtic, or simply Rhaetian. Their language merged with Latin to create Rhaeto-Romansch, which is still spoken in pockets of Switzerland. The Rhaetians may have been the earliest runemasters, for they left behind plenty of very runic-looking inscriptions on wood, bone, and stone. We know that the runes eventually made it north into the hands of the Germanic peoples, so it is not impossible that those Celts who would later be known as Gauls and Britons might have taken something of this ancient New Year's ritual with them when they left their old central European homeland. Could it have been that hint of lasciviousness, which characterized the Alpine Silvester, that lingered and later gave the English the idea that mistletoe was not, or ought not to be, allowed in church?

Because regional attitudes vary greatly, a few churches probably did deny entry to our little green-and-white friend, but most of them welcomed any plant that was still green in December, and not just in the aisles. Records indicate that in York, the mistletoe, like the ghostly bride who bears its name, made it all the way to the altar.

Juniper

(Juniperus communis)

In *Hänsel and Gretel*, the opera, the Nibbling Witch's wand is a juniper branch that she uses to "freeze" and "unfreeze" her household servants. This is not the first time a cleaning implement has been transformed into a magical instrument in the hands of a witch. While brooms were usually used to sweep the floor, juniper was burned to purify the general atmosphere of the home, especially at Christmastime. Like the blackthorn on St. Lucy's Eve, dried juniper cuttings were dropped over hot coals in a frying pan and walked through house and stables on the eves of Christmas and Epiphany. The fragrant white smoke purged the premises of pests both real (rats and fleas) and imagined (witches, ghosts, and goblins).

Juniper smoke may have given the Twelve Nights of Christmas their German name of *Rauhnächte*—*Rauh* coming from *Rauch*, or "smoke." Then again, *rauh* could mean "rough, hairy," referring to the werewolves and other furry characters prowling around at this time of year. (Werewolves, it must be noted, were believed to fear juniper trees.) *Rauh* can also mean "raw" as in "cold," as in *Rauhreif* or "hoarfrost," which is both cold and rough.

Juniper has an interesting relationship with the rowan, which was long used to discourage witches because they could not stomach the red berries. You might say that juniper and rowan get on like a house on fire, because that was exactly what would happen if you brought them inside together: your house would burn down. A sliver of juniper incorporated into a rowan wood boat, however, would prevent the boat from sinking.

In parts of Switzerland, boys still carry "brooms," poles topped with bunches of juniper, through the town on New Year's Eve, while in the Alps, Martinmas used to be the occasion to distribute *Gerten*, birch rods topped with clusters of oak leaves and juniper sprigs. The gerten were kept through the winter, then used to drive the cattle to the spring pastures. The more juniper berries that clung to the gerte, the more calves would be born in the spring.

Juniper thrives on the Lüneberg Heath in northern Germany, a former gathering place for witches. There, herds of *Heidschnucke*, "heath nibblers," an ancient breed of sheep, nibble everything but the sprawling juniper shrubs, which are much too prickly to be tasty. Another sort of spirit, gin, takes its name from the juniper berries (French *genièvre*) with which it is flavored. In the old days, a dash of gin on a silk handkerchief was the most elegant way to clean the surface of a mirror, so be sure to keep a bottle on hand if you plan to engage in any mirror magic on Christmas or New Year's Eve. (See also the Addendum in this book.)

Holly

(Ilex aquifolium)

One of the more obscure names for holly is "bat's wing." I'm sure my fellow bat-lovers will share my confusion as to why such a descriptive tag has not taken off. The holly's genus name, *Ilex*, was the Latin name for the holm oak (*Quercus ilex*), a Mediterranean oak whose dark green leaves do not turn brown even in winter. There are many mysteries concerning the holly, not the least of which is why so many people consider it to be so much holier than ivy. According to Christian legend, both the Cross and the Crown of Thorns were made of holly. For its crimes, God transformed the holly, which up till then had been a tall and stately palm, into a thorny shrub with berries red as blood. Even today, its German name is *Stechpalme*, or "prickly palm."

But holly as we know it was already among the greens with which the Romans dressed their homes for the pagan feast of Saturnalia. When you look at its history, the holly ought to top the list of disreputable Christmas trees (and shrubs), but except for a few vain attempts by early popes and Puritans, holly has never really fallen out of favor with the Church. It remains the shining Christmas star of the British Isles, in whose relatively mild climate this not-quite-so-cold-hardy evergreen thrives. From the early Middle Ages on, *hollen* was hauled into both churches and homes by the armful each December. It was best not to bring holly into the house until Christmas Eve, while holly gathered on Christmas Day would keep witches away. Domestic holly decorations had to be taken down and thrown away immediately after Twelfth Night, but church holly would attract good fortune all year.

Do not be mistaken: the holly is more than a good-time Christmas dandy. In the old days, poor householders in Wales would tie a generously leafy bunch of holly twigs in the middle of a long rope, the end of which the master of the house, having climbed up on the roof, would drop down the chimney. This was caught by the mistress, who took turns with him pulling the rope up and down until their makeshift chimney brush had scrubbed away the worst of the soot and sent it billowing out into the kitchen in an apocalyptic black cloud.[45]

A hobgoblin known as Charlie who haunted the kitchen of an inn on the Blackdowns of Somerset was partial to holly. Charlie liked to perch on the Clavey, a holly wood beam that hung above the fireplace and whose sole purpose was to give little Charlie a place to sit and warm his toes. Charlie was both a helpmeet and a mischievous imp. If he took against an expected guest, he would unset the table, putting all the cups and cutlery away before the guest arrived.

One of the most famous expected guests in English literature, the Ghost of Christmas Past, greets Scrooge with "a branch of fresh green holly in its hand," while the Ghost of Christmas Present wears a "holly wreath set here and there with shining icicles," reflecting, perhaps, the ancient Greek

45. See page 327 of John Seymour's *The Forgotten Arts and Crafts* for an enjoyable account of how Mr. Seymour and a neighbor attempted to unblock a Welsh farmhouse chimney on Old New Year's Day while still reeling from the excesses of Old New Year's Eve.

belief that holly could freeze water. Earlier on, the most famous of *un*expected Christmas guests, the Green Knight, shows up at King Arthur's court with a holly branch in one hand. (He has an axe in the other, much to the knights' chagrin.) The Blue Hag of the Scottish Highlands, meanwhile, kept her magic staff beneath a holly bush, which is why no grass will grow beneath a holly.

Ever since the Crucifixion, the holly has been associated with the condemned man or, more specifically, with his ghost. In the robber-ridden forest of Exmoor, there once grew a holly tree that cast a noose-shaped shadow on full moon nights. And in Yorkshire, the ghost of a man who had slain his own family was eventually caught in the holly's prickles.

Walter Calverley, Elizabethan master of Calverley Hall, murdered his wife and two of his children in a fit of pique after he had squandered his inheritance. He attempted to murder a third infant son but was waylaid and imprisoned at York Castle to await trial. Refusing to plead one way or the other, he was slowly pressed to death between a table and a heavy door, in accordance with the law. It has been suggested that by the time of his trial, the wretched Calverley had come to his senses and that his refusal to plead was a legal maneuver that allowed his surviving son to inherit what was left of the Calverley fortune. (Though it sounds a lot like "Calvary," the hill on which Jesus died, Calverley is actually an Old English name that refers to the use of calves in clearing the land.)

This final noble gesture was not enough to earn the wretched Walter rest. For a time, his ghost lingered in the lane outside Calverley village, where it behaved very much like a member of the Wild Hunt. Nearby Calverley Wood has been inhabited, or at least frequented, since the Bronze Age, as evinced by a large flat rock with numerous hollows and traces of circles pecked into it: a rather humble example of a cup-marked stone. Where there are cup marks, there are usually elves, and in the face of such a long human presence, the doomed man's spirit would have been subject to absorption by a host of preexisting traditions. His ghost was eventually subdued by the local vicar, who commanded it not to walk again so long as there were hollies growing in Calverley Wood.

Ivy

(Hedera helix)

On the old Norwegian stave calendar, St. Catherine's Day (November 25) was marked by a wheel, both in honor of the saint who was martyred on a spiked wheel and as a reminder that, if you hadn't already started, you had better get busy at the spinning wheel if you were to have all your yarn spun by the end of the Twelve Days of Christmas. In England, St. Catherine's Eve was the time to feast on cattern-cakes, large pastries shaped like wagon wheels, filled with honey, figs, mincemeat, or some other sticky stuff, decorated on top with ivy leaves. The masculine holly was frozen out of the festivities, since Cattern's Eve was a woman's holiday.

For the rest of the Christmas season, however, the ivy stood cold and shivering in the holly's shadow. From the medieval period onward, English homes, churches, and palaces were festooned with both holly and ivy, though the ivy was often made to stand out on the porch. Many believed it was bad luck to bring ivy indoors, for ivy wraps itself around old things, while holly always looks brand new. And a clump of holly does not look nearly as inviting to snakes and rats as a leafy bed of ivy does. While the ivy could not hope to compete with the robust red berries of the holly, the inclusion of ivy in a wreath of sterile holly would cancel out the bad luck inherent in the lack of fruits.

For all her evergreen appeal, the ivy has never quite been able to live down her work in the cemetery. A profusion of ivy on a virgin's grave meant that the occupant had pined away for love of a faithless fellow. Naturally, the survivor of such a dalliance would shun the ivy as a reminder of his guilt. On the other hand, the absence of ivy on someone's plot meant that his or her ghost did not lie quietly.

Lingonberry

(Vaccinium vitis-idaea)

Lingonberry is a low-lying evergreen shrub that bears small red berries and thrives in the lands of the northern lights. It is known in England as the cowberry, which is interesting in light of the bovine Lucia of West Gotland. In the old days, lingonberries were only gathered in the wild. Clement A. Miles, writing in 1912, identified the twigs in the Lucia crown as "whortleberry," that is, the dark blue-berried *Vaccinium myrtillis*, a.k.a. "bilberry," which is not an evergreen. Never having eaten at IKEA, Miles was probably unfamiliar with the lingonberry, which is also a beloved jam berry of the Swedes.

If you live outside Scandinavia, you probably do not have access to fresh lingonberry greens, in which case you can make your Lucia crown out of any other shrubby evergreen that won't prick the scalp. Since lingonberry is a member of the heath family, pagans, or "heathens," might prefer the etymological significance of using heather (*Calluna vulgaris*) instead. Incidentally, another English name for heather is "ling," from Old Norse *lyng*, suggesting that our ancestors were just as confused as we are.

Christmas Rose (1)

(Helleborus niger)

Though it looks like a delicate flower, the black hellebore, or Christmas rose, is an evergreen alpine perennial that not only over-winters but also blooms while there is still snow on the ground. It thrives throughout the high forests of central and southern Europe, but in Germany it grows wild only in Berchta's own country, the Berchtesgadener Alps, its flowers opening in the wake of the Buttnmandllauf. The leaves are dark green and leathery. The flower buds have a pinkish cast, but the five petals are an iridescent white upon opening.

The black hellebore most likely got its name from its brownish-black roots. Then again, it might take its name from the Black Plague, for the lanced buboes of plague victims were packed with a poultice made from these roots. One of the black hellebore's many German names is *Schwarzer Nieswurz*, or "black sneezing root," perhaps because a sneeze was often the first sign of the dreaded infection. The twelfth-century German abbess and visionary Hildegard of Bingen was aware of its medicinal properties, but since it is so highly poisonous, this Christmas rose is now exclusively an ornamental. In the Alps, it was also thought to be effective against plagues of witches. For this purpose, it was gathered on the first day of Christmas and strewn about the house. Meanwhile, the witches themselves used it as an ingredient in their flying ointment.

The first Christmas rose was supposed to have sprung from the tears of a poor girl who had nothing to give to the newborn Baby Jesus. Another legend tells of a beautiful maiden who, like Snow White, was cast out of her home to wander the snowbound forest. She must have caught something worse than a cold out there, for to save her, the goddess of the forest found it necessary to transform her into the white blossom of the black hellebore.

At one time, it was said, all the flowers in the forest bloomed on Christmas Eve. Now it is only the Christmas rose that, if all goes well, opens its petals at midnight. Watching it was a popular diversion on Christmas Eve, and the vigil continued in the dooryards of the Pennsylvania Dutch, who carried their *Christrose* with them to the New World. There it was eventually upstaged by the English holly, the practice dying out at the end of the nineteenth century. Back in Germany, the Christmas Rose continues to bloom throughout the season on greeting cards, napkins, and wrapping paper.

Christmas Rose (2)

(Anastatica hierochuntica)

Elsewhere in the Alps, the vigil takes place indoors and centers around another plant bearing the name of Christmas rose—a dry, dusty ball of tangled leaves. It is the *Anastatica hierochuntica*, also known as the Rose of Jericho or Resurrection Plant, in its dormant state. This Middle Eastern native that tumbles, rootless, along the desert floor, uncurls its long, thin leaves only during the rainy season, at which time the seeds at its heart quickly sprout and put out tiny white flowers. In Poschiavo, Switzerland, where it does not actually grow, this Christmas rose is set in a bowl of water early on Christmas Eve. It is then regaled with song. Just when the repertoire of carols is about to run out, which should happen around midnight, the previously desiccated plant opens its leaves, believing that spring has come to the Holy Land.

Christmas Rose (3)

(Rosa alba)

"Dead he is not," the Roses tell Gerda when she asks after the fate of her lost playmate Kay in Part the Third of Andersen's "The Snow Queen." "We have been down in the earth; the dead are there, but not Kay."

Gerda was neither the first nor the last unmarried girl to pump a rose for information about her beloved. Unlike our first two Christmas roses, this one is an actual member of the genus *Rosa*. In fact, you could use any kind of white rose, but because the following is a bit of antiquated English divination, it's probably best to use an old-fashioned Damask or Gallica rose. Whichever rose you choose, it must be white and you must pick it when the shadow on the sundial points sharply to noon on Midsummer Day, when the petals are fully open.

Do not put your rose in water. Wrap it in white tissue paper and place it at the back of a drawer until Christmas Day. When you get dressed on Christmas morning, choose something with a plunging neckline. Tuck the rose in your cleavage and go about your business. Sooner or later, someone will notice the crumpled flower and do you the favor of fishing it out. That someone is your future spouse.

Apple Tree

(Malus domestica)

To speak the Old English one-word phrase *Wassail* is to encourage the one you are addressing to "be of good health." To go "a-wassailing" is to travel about, wishing good health on everyone you meet. Not just people but orchards, fields, and even oxen could be wassailed. Most people have heard of the wassail bowl,[46] but there was also such a thing as a wassail box, in which a china baby doll rested inside a tissue paper nest, surrounded by apples and paper roses—a more than slightly creepy representation of the Baby Jesus. Wassailers might be rewarded, or urged to go away, with wassail cakes, beer, or money.

Wassailing took many forms, the most spectacular of which was the fire-wassail. This could take place anytime from Christmas Eve to Old Twelfth Eve. In eighteenth-century Herefordshire, in the barren winter fields, thirteen fires were kindled: one large, twelve small, like a fiery coven. In some parts of the county, these fires were indeed

46. Many assume that a wassail bowl must contain either hard or soft cider, but while hard cider was poured over the roots of the trees, the medieval wassail bowl, which was meant for human consumption, had no cider in it. Baked apples were floated in an ale-based concoction flavored with wine, sugar, and a host of spices. At the last minute, the hot brew was thickened with beaten eggs, thus making the traditional wassail bowl a cross between bishop's wine and eggnog.

identified as witches, while in others, they represented the twelve apostles and the Virgin Mary or someone named Old Meg. (Oddly enough, Jesus was left out of it.) The large fire might also be recognized as the sun, the smaller ones the months of the year. In Ross-on-Wye, a straw Maiden was also burned, perhaps as a bride for the Old Man we are soon to meet.

Another old West Country fire-wassail involved the burning of the Bush, a naked hawthorn branch whose twigs were bent into a globe. It hung in the farmhouse kitchen all year long but was taken down first thing on New Year's morning, when it was filled with straw and set alight. The blazing Bush was then carried—both quickly and carefully, one supposes—over the fields. The evil spirits who might cause the crops to wither would be trapped inside the globe and consumed along with the Bush. A new Bush was constructed immediately, the ends of the twigs singed in the fire of the old one, for it was not wise to go even one night without a Bush hanging in the kitchen. In Brinsop, the ceremony was concluded when all the men of the farm intoned the words "Auld Cider," deeply and droningly like Tibetan monks.

Cider brings us to the apple-wassail, or the "wassailing of the trees." This usually involved the splashing of the roots and trunk with hard cider, but it could also take a violent turn. On the Continent, the trees were stoned and/or beaten roundly with clubs and rods. Back in Herefordshire, the trees were wassailed with gunfire, but they were also regaled with song. In seventeenth-century Sussex, this was known as "howling the orchard," as in, "Stand fast root, bear well top/

Pray the God send us a howling good crop."[47] Many of the songs were addressed to "thee, old apple tree," or simply "old fellow," for special attention was always given to the oldest tree in the orchard.

The Apple-Tree Man, like the tomten in his botrae, resided in the oldest tree in the orchard, from which he was able to look after the farmer's fortunes. Every orchard had one. Going sometimes by the uncomplimentary nickname Lazy Lawrence, he discouraged thieves from making off with the apples at harvest time. In this he might be assisted by an elderly White Lady. In *Folktales of England*, Ruth L. Tongue contributes the Pitminster version of the following tale, in which a disinherited son prospers from a respectful encounter with the Apple-Tree Man.

According to the Somerset law of "Borough English," which is the opposite of primogeniture, the youngest son inherited lock, stock, and barrel. In this story, the youngest son rents his elder brother a patch of ground with a crumbling cottage on it, a stand of apple trees, and an ox and a donkey in their dotage. To add insult to injury, the lordly younger brother announces that he's going to drop by at midnight on Christmas Eve to force the donkey to tell him where on the property a certain treasure is supposed to be buried. It was widely believed that at midnight on Christmas Eve, animals were granted the power of speech, as they

47. All wassail-carol quotes in this paragraph were gleaned from pages 46–47 of Ronald Hutton's *The Stations of the Sun*. If you find yourself fascinated by wassailing customs, I recommend the chapter "Rituals of Purification and Blessing," in which those pages are contained, as well as Ella Mary Leather's classic tome, *The Folklore of Herefordshire*.

are in Beatrix Potter's *The Tailor of Gloucester*, the mice, birds, bats, and cats chattering away in nursery rhymes when the clock strikes twelve. The conversations of country livestock were more sinister, the horses, sheep, and cows sometimes uttering prophecies of death for those who dared to eavesdrop.

The elder brother goes out just before midnight on Christmas Eve to offer his last mug of cider to the trees. He's already given a few extra tidbits to the ox and the donkey and decorated their stalls with holly, so we know he's a decent fellow. As he pours the cider over the roots, the Apple-Tree Man appears to him, his face as wrinkled as that last frostbitten apple that was always left on the bough for the fairies. He urges the elder brother to poke a spade under one of his twisted roots. Sure enough, the elder brother unearths a chest full of gold coins, which he quickly hides inside the house before the younger brother arrives. As the younger brother turns in at the gate, he hears the donkey and the ox conversing about the rude and greedy fool who has come too late for the treasure he seeks. The younger brother returns home, outwitted by the Apple-Tree Man.

In "Tibb's Cat and the Apple-Tree Man," Ruth L. Tongue offers us another strange but charming tale about a curious little cat who resided at Tibb's Farm. This "dairymaid," as white tortoiseshell cats used to be called, wanted to know where the black cats went on all the "wisht nights witches do meet" and was always trying to follow them. Having failed to keep up on Candlemas and Halloween, on New Year's Eve she finally manages to reach the edge of the dark orchard into which the other cats have disappeared. But before she can put so much as a paw among the trees, the Apple-Tree Man calls out to her in his creaking voice, urging her to turn around and go back home, for soon the men will be coming to anoint his roots with cider and fire their guns to frighten the witches away. No, the orchard is no place for a little cat on New Year's Eve, he tells her. Best to wait and come back on St. Tibb's Eve. So the little cat went home to wait for St. Tibb's Eve, but it never came, and she soon forgot all about following the witches' cats.

Here's a final tip from the Apple-Tree Man: a December blossom, though pretty, means that someone in the household is going to die in January. And if there are blossoms while there are still ripe apples on the tree, pinch the blossoms off or, again, someone is sure to expire.

CONCLUSION

Eternity

There they sat, those two happy ones, grown up,
and yet children—children in heart, while all around
them glowed bright summer—warm, glorious summer.

~HANS CHRISTIAN ANDERSEN, "THE SNOW QUEEN"

By Candlemas, a full forty days will have passed since Christmas. Mary will have been churched,[48] so to speak; the days will have grown longer; and there will be little need for candles except from a spiritual point of view. On Candlemas Day, you can sit in a clean-swept parlor and watch the snowdrops opening outside the window, but tonight there is work to be done. "Down with the rosemary, and

48. Mary's postpartum purification at the Temple was the blueprint for the medieval Christian "churching" of women forty days after they had given birth.

so/Down with the bays and mistletoe"[49] and all the other Christmas greens: down they must come if you have not already stripped your mantels and banisters.

Nowadays, most of us are sparing with the greens, contenting ourselves with a wreath on the door and one waifish sprig of mistletoe hanging from the lintel. Swags and roping cost money, but back in the good old days when England was a maze of hedgerows, they were mostly free. At Christmastime, English churchwardens went a little wild, not so much with the rosemary and the bay—Mediterranean natives that must be cultivated—but with mistletoe, holly, ivy, broom, and box. It was largely English monks who ventured to the continent in the eighth and ninth centuries to stop the Germanic tribesmen worshipping among the trees or, worse yet, worshipping the trees themselves, so it's a little ironic that at Christmas the primeval forest should have reappeared inside the English church.

Most churches and homes had their decorations down by January 7, but it was permissible to leave them up until Candlemas. If you kept them up longer than that, you risked an infestation of undesirable spirits. For each leaf—some said needle or twig—of Christmas greenery lingering in the house after that date, there would be one goblin cavorting with the dust bunnies under the sofa or elsewhere in the house. But what to do with all those prickly things once they had been torn from their hooks and piled outside the door? The sheer volume of "brownery" was the perfect excuse for

49. These are the opening lines of Robert Herrick's 1670 poem "Ceremony upon Candlemas Eve," which is a short version of his "Ceremonies for Candlemas Eve."

a bonfire. This "Burning of the Greens" survives as a pyre built of Christmas trees in many American towns, especially in New England. In nineteenth-century Scotland, where there was little to be had in the way of Christmas greens, people observed Candlemas with bonfires of the yellow-flowered gorse and broom they gathered on the moor.

Judging by the number of crunchy brown wreaths still drooping on doors on Valentine's Day, it seems that people just don't worry about goblins anymore. I'd like to believe that this is because, on Candlemas, we're too busy enjoying one last hurrah to think about undecorating, but for most of us, this is not the case. In Mexico, *El Día de la Candelaria* is a day of fireworks and children's parties, and a few European countries hold candlelit processions, but these are the exceptions. Here in the twenty-first century, our lack of imagination has succeeded in banishing the ghosts, goblins, witches, and elves better than any bonfire could. By February 2, we have long since forgotten about Christmas and returned to the workaday world. With a full six weeks of winter still to get through, it's no wonder we get so excited about the prognostications of a certain groundhog.

Outside, beyond the snowdrops, the road salt dissolves the skin of ice only to be washed to the shoulder by the sweep of the spring rains. In July, the blacktop sends up shivers of heat so that, just for an instant, it looks as if there are tinsel streamers blowing on the horizon. And there we are, driving over the hot, treacly asphalt, petroleum fumes thick in the nose, entertaining memories of Christmas. Were we really visited by all those spirits, or was it just a dream? Ask the spirits themselves and they might tell us,

"Yes, it *was* all a dream," for, really, the spirits don't want to intrude: that is why they limit their visits to just a handful of days a year.

What would the children say if they could speak of such things? Most children rush headlong into Christmas without a care or backward glance. It's the others you want to watch: the boy who goes stiff and unsmiling as he's hoisted onto Santa's lap, the girl who approaches her stuffed stocking on Christmas morning with a sense of trepidation even though she can plainly see the doleful-eyed beanie baby staring out over the cuff. Those children *know*. That stocking, which appears unremarkable to adult eyes, has obviously been stuffed through supernatural agency and must therefore be handled with care. Once the toys have been unloaded and unwrapped, they will belong to the child, but until then, they belong to the Otherworld. Can't you see how the patterned Christmas paper, last handled by elves, still pulsates with magic? And what about the old man himself? How can he still be so spry, so *alive*, after two thousand years?

He can't be, not properly.

It's all right to accept presents from Santa Claus, these children would tell you, just as it was and is all right to accept gifts from the Christmas Child, Barborka, and Epiphany Witch, for these are our rewards, our incentives, for staying on our own side of the veil. It is patently *not* all right to wait up for the gift-giver, to sneak a peak under that screen of hair or bushel of tulle, or to follow the visitors out the door when they go. It is forbidden to dance with them, to eat at their table, and even, in some cases, to address them directly. The problem is not that the spirits *cannot* be engaged or looked upon in all their horror or glory, but that they *ought* not to be, not yet. If you have questions for them, if you would know more, you have only to wait a little—not an eternity, just the space of a lifetime.

ADDENDUM

A Calendar of Christmas Spirits and Spells

Mid-October to Mid-November: Álfablót

You don't have to wait for those mall decorations to go up to start celebrating the elves. Now is the time to host an Elf Sacrifice, or feast for the Álfar, in the old Nordic tradition.

November 11: St. Martin's Day

Don't be surprised if St. Martin has come and turned your bedside glass of water to wine in the night.

If the geese are ice-skating this morning, you'll have a mild winter. If they're splashing, you'll have a cold one. It's all up to the Wild Rider, who will be swirling through the skies on his dappled horse from now through the Twelve Nights of Christmas.

Jack-o'-lanterns are now out of season, but you might consider carving an old-fashioned turnip lantern in token of the bonfires that once burned on this night.

November 24: St. Catherine's Eve

If you're not too busy baking cattern-cakes, you should try to get a jump on your spinning today. All wool and flax must be spun by Twelfth Night if you are to have a good visit from the *Spinnstubenfrau.*

November 29: St. Andrew's Eve

All over northern Europe, this was the first of many nights on which *Bleigiessen*, the pouring of molten lead into cold water, might be practiced. Each hardened blob of lead was scrutinized for hints as to what gifts one might receive in the coming year. Does it resemble a coffin or a car? If you don't like what you see, you can try again on St. Barbara's, Christmas, New Year's, or Epiphany Eves. If you can't get your hands on a Bleigiessen kit—they're hard to come by these days—you can simply throw your shoes over your shoulder and see how they land.

Romanian vampires are out in force tonight: rub all window and door frames with garlic so they can't get in.

December 3: St. Barbara's Eve

You must go out and cut your "Barbara branches" tonight if they are to bloom in time for Christmas Eve. After you've put them in water, you can start looking out for the long-haired Barborky with their brooms, carpet-beaters, and baskets of sweets.

December 5: St. Nicholas' Eve

On this date in 1844, Hans Christian Andersen began writing "The Snow Queen" in his hotel room in Copenhagen.

Tomorrow, if St. Nicholas decides you have been good, you can start eating *Spekulaas*, "mirrors," which are cookies of pressed dough bearing images of windmills, castles, and seventeenth-century Dutch ladies. If he decides you have been bad, he will allow his sidekick Black Peter to stuff you in his sack and carry you off to Spain.

If Svatý Mikulaš, the Czech St. Nicholas, decides you have been naughty, he will turn you over to the goat-hoofed demon Čert, who will drag you all the way down to Hell.

Advent Thursdays

Advent candles are lit on the four Sundays preceding Christmas. (If Christmas Eve falls on a Sunday, it doubles as Fourth Advent.) The last three Thursdays of Advent were dedicated to Yuletide goddess/witch Berchta and her retinue. This was the time to scare evil spirits out from under the eaves by banging on pots and pans, playing fiddles, and throwing dried legumes. Spinning is forbidden on these nights.

In the Middle Ages, Advent, like Lent, was a season of abstinence. Sex at any time during Advent might result in a child who would eventually become a werewolf.

December 9: St. Anne's Day

In Sweden, the arrival of St. Anne's Day meant it was time to start reconstituting the dried cod that would be served on Christmas Eve. St. Anne is also popular with the Finns, who have conflated Jesus's maternal grandmother with their own female forest spirit, Anni. Today, Finnish women begin baking the Christmas loaves that will serve as centerpieces and, like the Swedish Yule Boar, ensure prosperity in the coming year.

December 12: St. Lucy's Eve

As well as marking the Old Style winter solstice, St. Lucy's Day was an Ember Day, or day of fasting, beginning the night before.

It's not yet time to deck the halls but to dust, scrub, and polish them in preparation for a visit from one of the many cross-dressing Slavic and Germanic Lucys.

On St. Lucy's Eve, young men might read their futures in the *Luzieschein*, balls of light dancing over the rooftops.

If you've started making Icelandic snowflake breads, better hide them from the ravenous Yule Lads, the first of whom arrives today.

December 13: St. Lucy's Day

Having survived the erstwhile darkest night of the year, you can get up early and celebrate Swedish style with "Lucy cats," coffee, and candlelight.

December 20: St. Thomas' Eve

In that region of the Czech Republic formerly known as Bohemia, this was not a good night to venture into the churchyard. At the stroke of twelve, all those who were called Thomas in life rose from their graves to be blessed by the dead saint himself, whose approach was heralded by the rumbling of his chariot wheels. At home, salt and holy water were cast about to petition the Apostle—Thor or Wodan in disguise?—for his protection.

Poor English children who went "a-thomassing," begging door to door on this night, were appeased with small change. In return, they handed out blessings in the form of holly and mistletoe sprigs.

Meanwhile, on the isle of Guernsey, will-o'-the-wisps, spectral dogs, and white rabbits (who were probably witches in disguise) were also about after dark. They haunted all the nights between St. Thomas' and New Year's Eve.

December 23

On this date in 1893, Engelbert Humperdinck's fairy opera *Hansel and Gretel* was performed for the first time.

December 24: Christmas Eve

Many Europeans are only just putting up their Christmas trees today. In some places, the Christ Child himself will bring the tree; in others, he/she will only light the candles.

Forget cookies for Santa; in Greece, tonight was the night to stuff the chimney full of pork sausages and sweetmeats for the kallikantzaroi. Try not to give birth today; a child born on Christmas Eve stands a good chance of becoming a kallikantzaros himself.

You should also put out some grain for the Yule Buck, fish heads for the Yule Boar, and, most importantly, don't forget the resident household sprite's annual bowl of rice porridge.

If you are staying home alone tonight, try not to fall asleep, and do not speak, no matter who or what comes in the door.

On Christmas Eve in Lithuania, unmarried young men and women might turn to catoptromancy, or mirror magic, to identify their future spouses. Banding together, they took a mirror to an abandoned (shall we read haunted?) house and lit two candles before it. The mirror would fog up, presumably from all that excited breathing going on in the unheated parlor, and as each participant wiped the mirror in turn, he or she would see the face of the person in question.

Christmas Eve was one of two nights of the year on which seals were most likely to shed their skins and appear in human form. The other was Midsummer's Eve.

December 25: Christmas Day

Reckoned by some as the First Day of Christmas (for others it is December 26), this is a relatively quiet day, supernaturally speaking. Scandinavians leaving for church before sunrise fit plenty of torches onto the sleigh to scare off any homeward-bound trolls they met along the way.

Holly picked today will keep witches away all year.

December 25 (or 26) to January 5 (or 6): The Twelve Days (and Nights) of Christmas

Do many of your neighbors go away over the Twelve Days of Christmas? If you notice a preponderance of wolves in the neighborhood at this time, then they probably haven't gone away at all; they've simply assumed lupine form, as werewolves are famous for doing between Christmas and

Epiphany. Children born during the Twelve Days of Christmas may become werewolves themselves.

In Alpine lands, these are the Smoky/Hairy/Rough Nights. Smudge all rooms of the house with incense or juniper boughs to smoke out the rough, hairy monsters abounding at this time.

December 31: New Year's Eve

This is Moving Night for Icelandic elves, so keep the Christmas lights twinkling and leave offerings of food outside the house. Those who decide to Sit Out at the crossroads and question the elves do so at their own risk.

Another curious feature of the old Icelandic New Year's Eve was "pantry drift": a magical white frost that trickled in through the pantry window, if it was left open, on the last night of the year. Pantry drift was supposed to taste like sugar and bring good fortune. If you wanted to partake of it, you had to stay up all night in the pantry and collect it in a pot. A cross had then to be placed over the mouth of the pot or the "drift" would disappear.

Midnight on New Year's Eve was the hour when a Finnish maiden might gaze into a candlelit mirror or, better yet, two mirrors placed opposite each other on a black cloth. There, she would hope to see the image of her future husband wandering in the uncertain light.

Stroke a piglet tonight, and you'll have good luck all next year.

Float a fresh ivy leaf in water inside a soup tureen on New Year's Eve. Put the lid on and don't disturb it until Twelfth Night (January 6). If the leaf remains green, you can look forward to a healthy year. If it is spotted, take comfort in the fact that reading ivy leaves is a notoriously unpredictable method of predicting the future.

January 1: New Year's Day

Be careful whom you let in the door first today. If you plan to interview first-footers ahead of time, look for tall, dark, handsome men, and remember to ask them if they were born feet first. Redheads need not apply.

Of course, if you can possibly arrange to have your chimney cleaned first thing today, that would be the best luck of all.

January 5: Epiphany Eve

Epiphany Eve is generally but not universally synonymous with Twelfth Night. If you counted Christmas Day as the First Day of Christmas, then Twelfth Night will fall on the night of January 5. If, however, you didn't receive your partridge in a pear tree until December 26, then Twelfth Night is January 6.

At Epiphany, homeowners in eastern and central Europe chalk a magically protective formula over the doors of their homes. It consists of the century followed by the initials of the Three Kings—Kaspar, Melchior, and Balthasar—ending with the year: e.g., 20K + M + B13. Before the Three Kings rose to fame, it was the Drudenfuss or pentagram that was chalked on the lintel.

In Lithuania, the girl who could stare at the moon's face for a full hour on the Eve of Epiphany, then wash for another hour before retiring to bed, would be rewarded by a visit from a white ghost. The ghost would answer whatever questions she cared to ask it, including, no doubt, whom she would marry and when.

Just when you thought it was safe to go outside again, the Nordic Yule Buck is back, capering behind the Star Boys in the village street.

Any lingering elves should be moving along today. Take down your Christmas decorations, and they'll probably take the hint.

If your stocking wasn't filled on Christmas Eve, you can hang it up tonight and the Italian witch Befana will do the job.

Stick to fish, pancakes, or dumplings for dinner on Epiphany Eve or run the risk of Frau Berchta coming and slitting open your stomach.

If you have apple trees, anoint the roots of the oldest one with hard cider. Pinch off any unseasonal blossoms but leave one apple on the tree for the fairies or the Apple-Tree Man.

January 6: Epiphany or Twelfth Night

Today is *Perchtentag* in Austria. Represented by both her pretty and ugly servants, our White Witch, Perchta, has her last hurrah.

January 13: St. Knut's Day

Scandinavians take down their Christmas trees today. The Yule Buck comes knocking once more in the form of *Nuuttipukki*, the Finnish St. Knut's Day Goat-man. Offer him beer in return for a final blessing.

February 2: Candlemas

This is your very last chance to take down your Christmas decorations, green or otherwise. If you keep them up any longer, then you probably deserve anything the goblins can dish out!

St. Tibb's Eve

If you've made it through the whole Christmas season and still haven't seen any witches, best to go home and wait for St. Tibb's Eve.

Glossary

aspergillum: a sort of holy watering can or wand. The original meaning of the word *aspersion* was a "sprinkling or scattering of water or dust." The purpose of an aspergillum is to cast holy water, not aspersions, over church, altar, home, and people alike. An aspergillum may be a fancy vessel or be as simple as a brush or leafy twig for dipping in the water.

aurora borealis: Latin, "dawn of the north wind." See also *northern lights*.

Balkans: mountainous region north of Greece containing the nations of Croatia, Bosnia-Herzegovina, Serbia, Montenegro, Albania, Macedonia, and Bulgaria. The Balkan languages belong to the South Slavic family, except for Albanian, which is descended from ancient Illyrian.

Baltic: area of northeastern Europe at the easternmost end of the Baltic Sea. Although Germany, Denmark, Finland, Sweden, and Poland have their own stretches of Baltic coastline, the term is used to refer to the language, traditions, and ancient religions of Latvia, Lithuania, and Estonia. Estonian, like Sami, belongs to the Finno-Ugric family of languages, while Latvian and Lithuanian cling to their own ancient branch of the Indo-European family tree, Baltic.

boggart: tutelary, and sometimes troublesome, English house ghost, most often heard but not seen.

box: evergreen shrub with tiny, shiny green leaves that lends itself especially well to topiary. The kind you are probably used to seeing at the edges of well-kept garden paths is actually the slow-growing dwarf or "Dutch" variety; non-dwarf varieties of *Buxus sempervirens* can grow to thirty feet. In addition to votive figures, the wood, which is smooth and hard, was used to make lutes, printing blocks, and—you guessed it—boxes.

broom: the common, or Scotch, broom, *Cytisus scoparius*, whose yellow flowers brighten the moors in springtime. Just as boxes were once made from boxwood, brooms were often bundles of broom twigs. Meanwhile, "butcher's broom," *Ruscus aculeatus,* a.k.a "box holly," was sometimes commandeered as a Christmas green because it bore red berries in December.

Counter-Reformation: the Catholic Church's answer to the Protestant Reformation. Also known as the "Catholic Revival," it lasted from 1542 to 1648 and focused on the proper education of priests as well as a return to spirituality and mysticism. See also *Reformation*.

creosote: the deposit left behind by the burning of wood or coal.

distaff: a stick that, in the thread-making process, acts as the hand-spinner's third hand. The distaff holds the fluff of unspun fibers that the spinner draws out and feeds to the whirling spindle controlled by the other hand. The distaff eventually became part of that newfangled invention, the spinning wheel, but hand-held distaffs and spindles remained in use for a long time because they were portable: you can't take a spinning wheel into the pasture or along the road to market.

Elizabethan: pertaining to the reign of Queen Elizabeth I, who ruled England from 1558 to 1603.

Ember Days: fasting days, occurring one in each season, in the medieval liturgical year. "Ember" here has nothing to do with fireplace embers; the name comes from the Old English *ymbrendagas*, meaning "periodic days," because they occur periodically throughout the year. The other Ember Days are the Wednesday following Ash Wednesday, Whitsunday (Pentecost, the seventh Sunday after Easter), and Autumn Crouchmas (September 14). Those born on Ember Days were supposed to be able to see spirits.

Finnic: non-Indo-European family of languages belonging to the broader Finno-Ugric family. The Finnic languages include Finnish, Sami, and Estonian.

flax: *Linum usitatissimum*, a tall, willowy annual whose stems are the source of both fine linen and of the coarser byproduct, tow. If you are "flaxen-haired," your hair resembles the stem's fine, pale inner fibers, which were spun into thread. The flax plant bears delicate, light blue flowers and hard, round seeds, known as linseed.

flue: a passage that conducts the smoke from the fireplace or grate up into the main chimney.

Glückspilz: German for "lucky mushroom," the *Amanita muscaria* or fly agaric. The fly agaric has a fat white stalk, red cap, and white spots. Also known as "the little man of the forest," the image of this hallucinogenic and highly poisonous fungus is an intrinsic part of the German Christmas celebration.

goblin: an ugly, mischievous spirit not unlike a troll, though perhaps smaller. The word *goblin* comes from Old French *gobelin* rather than German *kobold*. Both words, however, stem from the Greek *kobalos*, a mischievous spirit.

gorse: *Ulex europaeus*, a thorny shrub of the moors. Unlike its fellow heath-dweller the common broom (see *broom*), which blooms only in springtime, gorse keeps its cheerful yellow blossoms going all year long. Gorse also answers to the names "furze" and "whin."

Green Knight: a.k.a. "Knight of the Green Chapel," anti-hero of the fourteenth-century Middle English chivalric romance *Sir Gawain and the Green Knight*. Because he is green-skinned, carries a holly branch, and survives decapitation, many take him for a pre-Christian Celtic vegetal spirit.

Hidden Folk: the *landvaettir*, or aboriginal land spirits of Iceland. When the Norse arrived in Iceland, there were no elves or *Álfar* on the island, but there were plenty of hidden, or *huldre*, folk. Soon after settlement, the place started filling up with "elves" as well, and the two terms are now used interchangeably by most translators.

howe: a burial mound, especially one that is so old that no one can remember who is actually buried in it. Howes are usually supposed to contain royal bones and treasure. In England, they are also known as "lows" or "barrows," but one is only ever laid "in howe."

Ilsenstein: now *Ilsestein*, a barren granite mountaintop poking out of the Harz forest in the German state of Sachsen-Anhalt. An iron cross was installed at its summit in 1814, but this did not seem to deter Hansel and Gretel's Nibbling Witch, who lived at its foot. "Ilse" is a German girl's name, which begs the question, "Who was Ilse?" According to one legend, she was the daughter of a knight whose castle stood on the nearby Westerberg. In another, her father was the *Brockengespenst*, a giant similar in appearance to the Green Knight but who carried a fir tree instead of a holly branch. In any case, the beautiful Ilse was turned to stone as the result of a love triangle involving herself, a tricky young journeyman, and the resident witch's daughter, Yellow Trudi.

Jacobean: pertaining to the reign of King James I, who ruled England from 1603 to 1625. *James* is the English form of the medieval Spanish *Jayme*, which comes from *Jacobus*, which is the Latin form of the Hebrew *Ya'aqob*.

kota: a traditional, tipi-like Sami dwelling that can be set up wherever the reindeer are grazing. In "The Snow Queen," both the Finmark woman's and Lapland woman's houses resemble the *kota* in that the roofs slope all the way to the ground. Because the Finmark woman's house has no door, Gerda must knock at the chimney.

Lucifer: Latin for "light-bringing," instigator of an angelic revolt in heaven, more or less synonymous with Satan, but also used to denote Venus in its role of morning star. The name *Lucia* also means "light-bringer."

Magi: plural of *Magus*, priests of the Zoroastrian religion of ancient Persia. In popular Greek imagination, the Magi were skilled sorcerers, astrologers, and mirror-gazers—how else would they have known to follow the Star of Bethlehem? See also *Three Kings*.

Moor: name given by Europeans to an Arabic-speaking person of northwestern Africa or early medieval Spain. The name "Moor" comes from Greek *mauros*, meaning "black, dark," and, in fact, the Moor was usually represented as a sub-Saharan African rather than an actual Arab or Berber. The character of the dark-skinned Moor added a note of exoticism to medieval pageants and theatre pieces. The most famous Moor of all is Othello, the humblest Black Peter.

moor: treeless land unsuitable for farming on which such low, scrappy shrubs as heather, broom, gorse, and juniper may thrive.

mumming: costumed cavorting, often door to door, with the participants (mummers) taking care to disguise their identities. Like trick-or-treaters, mummers must be paid off with food, drink, or money. Unlike trick-or-treaters, mummers are usually adults and often perform a short play at each stop.

norns: a class of supernatural women in Norse mythology, the most famous of whom were Urd, Verdandi, and Skuld, who sat spinning the threads of destiny at the foot of the World Tree.

northern lights: the aurora borealis—officially, a phenomenon caused by electrical sparks tossed about on the solar wind. Unofficially, there is little agreement about the source of this arctic show of lights. In Lapland, they are said to be the dancing souls of the happy dead, the restless souls of the *un*happy dead, and the switching tail of a celestial fox. Although green often dominates in photographs, the northern lights actually come in a whole range of colors. In one of his letters to J. R. R. Tolkien's children, Father Christmas paints the "Rory Bory Aylis" as a fiery rainbow, though he admits to not having done it properly. Out of respect for the phenomenon's auditory component—a sort of crackling hiss—the Sami make a point of observing the northern lights in silence. (In "The Snow Queen," Andersen would have the lights say, "Isch! isch!" as if "the sky was sneezing.")

Picts: ancient natives of northern Scotland who, in lieu of clothes, tattooed or painted themselves blue and apparently spoke a language unrelated to any other. The Picts' air of mystery probably stems from the fact that their homeland lay north of Hadrian's Wall, a region too cold and damp for the Roman recorders to venture into. All in all, the Picts, who had their own kingdom until AD 843, were probably not much different from their Celtic neighbors. The Picts had their own robust, curving artistic style and, judging by the artifacts they left behind, liked to make pictures on stones and silver jewelry as much as on themselves.

pitch: a sticky black substance distilled from pine wood, almost, but not quite, the same thing as tar. In the fairy tale "Mother Hulda" (German *Frau Holle*), pitch is poured over the stepsister's head. "Pitch" is the translation of the German *Pech*, but I think the Grimms should have used *Teer*, or "tar," which is much easier to pour over someone's head. Pitch oozes slowly enough that even a lazybones probably could have dodged it and gotten away scot-free. The German *Pech* means "bad luck" as well as "pitch." The opposite of *Pech* is *Schwein*, which denotes both a pig and a stroke of uncommonly good luck. See also *tar*.

primogeniture: the practice of bequeathing all one's worldly goods to the eldest son.

primstav: "prime staff," the Norwegian stave calendar, a long, flat stick on which feast days and dates of agricultural importance were marked by pictograms. Most Scandinavian stave calendars also employed runes and required specialized knowledge to read.

Puck: see *Robin Goodfellow*.

Ragnarök: also *Ragnarøkkr*, in Norse mythology, the violent, fiery End of the World, gods and all (though a few chess pieces survive). Ragnarök is really nothing to worry about, because a new world will spring up immediately in the old one's place.

reel: a four-to-six-spoked rimless wheel on which spun thread was wound into a skein. The rotary flax wheel on which thread could be easily wound from the bobbin was not introduced until the 1700s. The handheld skein-winders of earlier centuries were much quieter, so it's anybody's guess how Frau Holle might have made the thunder back in the Middle Ages. It's possible she left it to Thor.

Reformation: religious movement initiated by Martin Luther's nailing of his "Ninety-Five Theses on the Power and Efficacy of Indulgences" to a church door in Wittenberg, Germany, in 1517. Rather than achieving Luther's goal of reforming the Catholic Church, the Reformation gave rise to the many Protestant denominations we have today. German legend credits Luther with putting up the first Christmas tree.

risir: in Norse mythology, a class of primordial giants who were supposed to be especially beautiful.

Robin Goodfellow: a.k.a. "Puck," a helpful, yet mischievous, English sprite. He would enter the house at night to do such chores as sweep the floor and grind flour, mustard seeds, or barley grains for beer. In return, he accepted milk and bread but never clothes.

skyr: a homemade, Icelandic yogurt-like dairy product. The making of skyr, along with an older form of the language and a passionate belief in elves, is one of those cultural artifacts that have been kept up in Iceland long after they died out in the rest of Scandinavia.

tar: a black, oozy substance distilled from pine roots. When all the tar and pitch have been drawn from the wood, all that remains is that other essential ingredient of Christmas: charcoal. Tar, which smells strongly of turpentine, was used for waterproofing boats and wooden buildings as well as for sticking feathers to unfortunate humans.

Thor: thunderer, giant-killer, red-bearded son of Odin and the earth goddess Jörd. Though unskilled in magic, Thor was one of the most popular Norse gods, especially outside the aristocracy. He got out of most scrapes by laying about him with the double-headed hammer Mjölnir, the image of which was employed by his worshippers as a talisman and mark of the god's cult. Thor drove a cart pulled by two goats that could be killed and eaten, then put back together and made to pull the cart again.

Three Kings: Kaspar (or Caspar), Melchior, and Balthasar, who followed the Star westward to Bethlehem in order to present gifts to the Baby Jesus. In Spain and Latin America, it is the Three Kings who bring gifts to children on Epiphany Eve. See also *Magi*.

tow: the shorter, coarser fibers left over from the working of flax into linen thread. If you are "tow-headed," your hair resembles these coarser blond strands that were used to make rope, ship's caulking, wigs, and false beards. See also *flax*.

Turkish delight: a confection consisting of gluey hunks of rosewater and almonds or pistachios dusted with powdered sugar. Personally, I would be horrified to find a box of Turkish delight in my stocking no matter how prettily it was wrapped, but I may be alone in this. Slabs of Turkish delight form the roof of the witch's house in *Hansel and Gretel*, and the confection is the principal means by which the White Witch gains Edmund's confidence when he first arrives in Narnia. (When Father Christmas is finally able to make his way into that land, he conjures the humbler treat of a pot of tea with cream and lump sugar.)

warp: the set of vertical threads that must be carefully assembled on the frame of the loom before weaving can begin. Once the loom has been "warped," the weft (also "woof"), or horizontal threads, can be inserted to achieve the desired pattern.

Bibliography

Books

Andersen, Hans Christian. *Hans Christian Andersen: The Complete Fairy Tales and Stories*. Translated by Erik Christian Haugaard. New York: Anchor Books, 1983.

———. *Tales from Hans Andersen*. New York: Thomas Y. Crowell and Company (very old: no copyright or translator name).

Andrew, Peter, ed. *Christmas in Today's Germany*. Chicago: World Book Encyclopedia, Inc., 1974.

Árnadóttir, Hólmfrídur. *When I Was a Girl in Iceland*. Boston: Lothrop, Lee and Shepard Co., 1919.

Barber, Elizabeth Wayland. *Women's Work: The First 20,000 Years: Women, Cloth and Society in Early Times*. New York: W. W. Norton and Company, 1994.

Barber, Paul. *Vampires, Burial, and Death*. New Haven, CT: Yale University Press, 2010.

Bates, Brian. *The Real Middle Earth: Magic and Mystery in the Dark Ages.* London: Pan Books, 2002.

Bjornsson, Arni. *Icelandic Feasts and Holidays: Celebrations, Past and Present.* Translated by May and Hallberg Hallmundsson. Reykjavik, Iceland: Iceland Review, 1980.

Boucher, Alan. *Elves, Trolls and Elemental Beings: Icelandic Folktales II.* Reykjavik, Iceland: Iceland Review, 1981.

Branston, Brian. *The Lost Gods of England.* London: Thames and Hudson, 1957.

Briggs, Katharine M. *The Fairies in Tradition and Literature.* London: Routledge and Kegan Paul, 1967. (Republished by Routledge Classics, 2002.)

Briggs, Katharine M., and Ruth L. Tongue, eds. *Folktales of England.* Chicago: University of Chicago Press, 1965.

Cagner, Ewert, ed. *Swedish Christmas.* New York: Henry Holt and Company, 1959. (First published in Sweden in 1954.)

Christiansen, Reidar, ed. *Folktales of Norway.* Translated by Pat Shaw Iverson. Chicago: The University of Chicago Press, 1964.

Crain, Mary Beth. *Haunted Christmas: Yuletide Ghosts and Other Spooky Holiday Happenings.* Guilford, CT: Globe Pequot Press, 2010.

Dasent, George Webbe. *The Cat on the Dovrefell: A Christmas Tale.* New York: G. P. Putnam's Sons, 1979.

Davidson, Hilda Ellis. *Gods and Myths of the Viking Age.* New York: Bell Publishing Company, 1981.

———. *Roles of the Northern Goddess.* New York: Routledge, 1988.

De Paola, Tomie. *The Legend of Old Befana*. New York: Harcourt, Brace, Jovanovich, 1980.

Dery, Dominika. *The Twelve Little Cakes*. New York: Riverhead Books, 2004.

Dickens, Charles. *A Christmas Carol*. New York: Macmillan, 1966.

Ellis, Hilda Roderick. *The Road to Hel: A Study of the Conception of the Dead in Old Norse Literature*. New York: Greenwood Press, 1968.

Fertig, Terry. *Christmas in Denmark*. Chicago: World Book Encyclopedia, Inc., 1986.

Fertig, Theresa Kryst. *Christmas in the Netherlands*. Chicago: World Book-Childcraft International, Inc., 1981.

Frazer, Sir James George. *The Golden Bough*, abridged edition. New York: Collier Books, 1922.

Gardner, Gerald B. *Witchcraft Today*. New York: The Citadel Press, 1955.

Gaster, Theodor. *New Year: Its History, Customs and Superstitions*. New York: Abelard-Schuman, 1955.

Giblin, James Cross. *Chimney Sweeps*. New York: T. Y. Crowell, 1982.

Griffin, Robert H., and Ann H. Shurgin, eds. *The Folklore of World Holidays*, 2nd ed. Detroit, MI: Gale Research, 1999.

Grimm Brothers. *Household Stories*. Translated by Lucy Crane. New York: Dover Publications, 1963.

Grimm, Jacob. Translated by James Steven Stallybrass. *Teutonic Mythology, Volumes I–III*. London: George Bell and Sons, 1883. (Republished by Dover Books, 2004.)

———. *Teutonic Mythology, Volume IV*. London: George Bell and Sons, 1888. (Republished by Dover Books, 2004.)

Grossman, John. *Christmas Curiosities: Odd, Dark, and Forgotten Christmas*. New York: Stewart, Tabori and Chang, 2008.

Hall, John Oscar. *When I Was a Boy in Norway*. Boston: Lothrop, Lee & Shepard, 1921.

Halpert, Herbert and G. M. Story, eds. *Christmas Mumming in Newfoundland*. Toronto: University of Toronto Press, 1969.

Hole, Christina. *Haunted England: A Survey of English Ghost-Lore*. London: B. T. Batsford, 1940.

Horsfield, Margaret. *Biting the Dust: The Joys of Housework*. New York: St. Martin's Press, 1998.

Hughes, Ellen. *Christmas in Finland*. Chicago: World Book, Inc., 2001.

Hutton, Ronald. *Shamans: Siberian Spirituality and the Western Imagination*. London: Hambledon and London, 2001.

———. *The Stations of the Sun: A History of the Ritual Year in Britain*. New York: Oxford University Press, 1996.

Keightley, Thomas. *The World Guide to Gnomes, Fairies, Elves, and Other Little People*. New York: Gramercy Books, 2000.

Klobuchar, Lisa. *Christmas in Switzerland*. Chicago: World Book, Inc., 1995.

Kretzenbacher, Leopold. *Santa Lucia und die Lutzelfrau*. Munich, Germany: Verlag R. Oldenbourg, 1959.

Larson, Katherine. *The Woven Coverlets of Norway*. Seattle: University of Washington Press, 2001.

Leach, Maria, ed. *Funk and Wagnalls Standard Dictionary of Folklore, Mythology and Legend*. New York: Funk and Wagnalls, 1949.

Leather, Ella Mary. *The Folklore and Witchcraft of Herefordshire*. Church Stretton, England: Oakleaf Books, 2004. (Abridged from *The Folklore of Herefordshire*, first published in Hereford, England, by Jakeman and Carver, 1912.)

Lecouteux, Claude. *Phantom Armies of the Night*. Translated by Jon E. Graham. Rochester, VT: Inner Traditions, 2011.

Lewis, C. S. *The Lion, the Witch and the Wardrobe*. New York: Macmillan, 1950.

———. *Prince Caspian*. London: G. Bles, 1951.

Lindahl, Carl, John McNamara, and John Lindow, eds. *Medieval Folklore: A Guide to Myths, Legends, Tales, Beliefs and Customs*. New York: Oxford University Press, 2002.

Lindow, John. *Norse Mythology: A Guide to the Gods, Heroes, Rituals, and Beliefs*. New York: Oxford University Press, 2001.

The Mad Pranks and Merry Jests of Robin Goodfellow: Reprinted from the Edition of 1628. With an Introduction by J. Payne Collier. London: C. Richards, 1841.

McEwan, Graham J. *Mystery Animals of Britain and Ireland*. London: Robert Hale, 1986.

McLenighan, Valjean. *Christmas in Austria*. Chicago: World Book Encyclopedia, Inc., 1982.

Magnusson, Magnus, and Hermann Palsson, trans. *Njal's Saga*. London: Penguin, 1960.

———. *Laxdaela Saga*. London: Penguin, 1969.

Manker, Ernst. *People of Eight Seasons: The Story of the Lapps*. Translated by Kathleen McFarlane. New York: The Viking Press, 1964.

Maple, Eric. *The Realm of Ghosts*. New York: A. S. Barnes and Company, 1964.

———. *Supernatural England*. Abbey Chambers, England: Fraser Stewart Books, 1977.

Marboe, Ernst. *Das Österreichbuch*. Vienna, Austria: Verlag der Österreichischen Staatsdruckerei, 1948.

Masefield, John. *The Box of Delights*. New York: New York Review of Books, 2007. ("This text, newly corrected from the manuscript by Philip W. Errington." First published in 1935.)

Metzger, Christine, ed. *Culinaria Germany*. Cologne, Germany: Koennemann, 2000.

Miles, Clement A. *Christmas Customs and Traditions: Their History and Significance*. New York: Dover Books, 1976. (Unabridged republication of the work originally published by T. Fisher Unwin in 1912 under the title *Christman in Ritual and Tradition, Christian and Pagan*.)

Moore, Clement. *'Twas the Night Before Christmas: A Visit from St. Nicholas*. New York: Houghton Mifflin, 1912.

Neumuller, Anders. *God Jul: A Swedish Christmas*. New York: Skyhorse Publishing, 2009.

Ojakangas, Beatrice. *The Great Scandinavian Baking Book*. Boston: Little, Brown and Company, 1988.

Poole, Gray Johnson. *Mistletoe: Fact and Folklore*. New York: Dodd, Mead and Company, 1976.

Porteous, Alexander. *The Forest in Folklore and Mythology*. New York: Macmillan, 1928.

Potter, Beatrix. *The Tailor of Gloucester*. New York: Frederick Warne & Co., 1903.

Purkiss, Diane. *At the Bottom of the Garden: A Dark History of Fairies, Hobgoblins, and Other Troublesome Things*. New York: New York University Press, 2000.

Raetsch, Christian, and Claudia Mueller-Ebeling. *Pagan Christmas*. Translated from the German by Katja Lueders. Rochester, VT: Inner Traditions, 2006.

Rieti, Barbara. *Strange Terrain: The Fairy World in Newfoundland*. St. John's, NL: Institute of Social and Economic Research, Memorial University of Newfoundland, 1991.

Riis, Jacob. *The Old Town*. New York: The Macmillan Company, 1909.

Roback, Charles W. *The Mysteries of Astrology and the Wonders of Magic*. Boston: Published by the author, 1854.

Ross, Corinne. *Christmas in Britain*. Chicago: World Book Encyclopedia, Inc., 1978.

———. *Christmas in Italy*. Chicago: World Book Encyclopedia, Inc., 1979.

———. *Christmas in Scandinavia*. Chicago: World Book Encyclopedia, Inc., 1977.

Rowling, J. K. *Harry Potter and the Half-Blood Prince*. New York: Arthur A. Levine Books, 2005.

———. *Harry Potter and the Prisoner of Azkaban.* New York : Arthur A. Levine Books, 1999.

Russ, Jennifer M. *German Festivals and Customs.* London: Oswald Wolff, 1982.

Rydberg, Viktor. *The Christmas Tomten.* Freely adapted by Linda M. Jennings from a translation from the Swedish by Lone Thygesen Blecher and George Blecher. New York: Coward, McCann & Geoghegan, 1981.

Saxo Grammaticus. *The History of the Danes: Books I–IX.* Edited by Hilda Ellis Davidson, translated by Peter Fisher. Rochester, NY: D. S. Brewer, 2008.

Scherf, Gertrud. *Zauberpflanzen, Hexenkraeuter: Mythos und Magie heimischer Wild- und Kulturpflanzen.* (Enchanted Plants, Witches' Herbs: Myth and Magic of Indigenous Wild and Cultivated Plants.) Munich, Germany: BLV, 2003.

Seymour, John. *The Forgotten Arts and Crafts.* New York: Dorling Kindersley, 2001.

Shoemaker, Alfred L. *Christmas in Pennsylvania: A Folk-Cultural Study, 50th Anniversary Edition.* Mechanicsburg, PA: Stackpole Books, 2009.

Siefker, Phyllis. *Santa Claus, Last of the Wild Men: The Origins and Evolution of Saint Nicholas, Spanning 50,000 Years.* Jefferson, NC: McFarland and Company, 1997.

Simpson, Jacqueline. *Icelandic Folktales and Legends.* Berkeley: University of California Press, 1972.

Spicer, Dorothy Gladys. *Festivals of Western Europe.* New York: H. W. Wilson, 1958.

Sturluson, Snorri. *Heimskringla: or, Lives of the Norse Kings.* Translated by Erling Monsen and A. H. Smith. Mineola, NY: Dover Publications, 1990.

———. *The Prose Edda.* Translated by Jesse L. Byock. New York: Penguin, 2005.

Swanton, Michael J., trans. and ed. *The Anglo-Saxon Chronicle.* New York: Routledge, 1998.

Thompson, Martha Wiberg, ed. *Superbly Swedish: Recipes and Traditions.* Iowa City, IA: Penfield Press, 1983.

Thorsson, Onolfur, ed. *The Sagas of the Icelanders: A Selection.* New York: Viking, 1997.

Tolkien, J. R. R., edited by Baillie Tolkien. *Letters from Father Christmas.* Boston: Houghton Mifflin, 1999.

Tongue, R. L. *Somerset Folklore.* London: The Folk-Lore Society, 1965.

Westwood, Jennifer, and Jacqueline Simpson. *The Lore of the Land: A Guide to England's Legends, from Spring-Heeled Jack to the Witches of Warboys.* London: Penguin, 2005.

Wullschlager, Jackie. *Hans Christian Andersen: The Life of a Storyteller.* New York: Alfred A. Knopf, 2001.

Other

"Czech Christmas." Prague Information Service 2009. www.praguecityline.com.

Fox, Amanda. "Christmas Traditions and Celebrations in Iceland." Helium, 2002–2010. www.helium.com.

"Hansel and Gretel: a Fairy Opera in Three Acts." The Internet Archive. www.archive.org/stream/hnselgretelfai00humpvoft_dvjv.txt.

Haslam, Garth. "The Green Children." www.anomalyinfo.com.

Ilic, Erin N. "Creepy Christmas," *Early American Life*, Christmas 2010.

Kiefer, Thomas J. "Wienechts-Chindli." www.fotocommunity.de.

Kodratoff, Yves. "Voluspa: The Predictions of the Prophetess, Old Norse and English Versions with Commentary." Nordic Magic Healing: 1998. www.nordic-life.org.

"Lapland." *The Encyclopedia Britannica*, 11th ed., vol. XVI. New York: The Encyclopedia Britannica Company, 1911.

"Lithuanian Customs and Traditions." http://ausis.gf.vu.lt/eka/customs/tradc.html.

Rumpf, Marianne, Anthony Hellenberg, and Elizabeth Tucker. "Legends of Bertha in Switzerland," *Journal of the Folklore Institute*, volume 14, no. 3. Bloomington: Indiana University Press, 1977.

"Tales of the White Lady." Tales and Legends of Český Krumlov Castle, 2006–2007. State Castle Český Krumlov. www.castle.ckrumlov.cz.

Velinger, Jan. "Perchta of Rozmberk—The White Lady of Bohemia." Radio Prague: February 4, 2004. http://www.radio.cz/en/section/czechs/perchta-of-rozmberk-the-white-lady-of-bohemia.

Vilnius-Life.com. "A Royal Romance." www.vilnius-life.com/vilnius/barbara-radziwill.

Index

C

G

T

To Write to the Author

If you wish to contact the author or would like more information about this book, please write to the author in care of Llewellyn Worldwide Ltd. and we will forward your request. Both the author and publisher appreciate hearing from you and learning of your enjoyment of this book and how it has helped you. Llewellyn Worldwide Ltd. cannot guarantee that every letter written to the author can be answered, but all will be forwarded. Please write to:

Linda Raedisch
℅ Llewellyn Worldwide
2143 Wooddale Drive
Woodbury, MN 55125-2989.

Please enclose a self-addressed stamped envelope for reply, or $1.00 to cover costs. If outside the USA, enclose an international postal reply coupon.